Formalised Access to Pre-jurisdictional Free Legal Aid

Ius, Lex et Res Publica
Studies in Law, Philosophy and Political Cultures

Edited by Barbara Janusz-Pohl and Anna Jaron

Volume 27

Bogusław Przywora / Aleksander Wróbel

Formalised Access to Pre-jurisdictional Free Legal Aid.

Analysis based on Example of Ukraine, Poland, Great Britain and Sweden.

PETER LANG

Lausanne · Berlin · Bruxelles · Chennai · New York · Oxford

Bibliographic Information published by the Deutsche Nationalbibliothek
The Deutsche Nationalbibliothek lists this publication in the Deutsche Nationalbibliografie; detailed bibliographic data is available online at http://dnb.d-nb.de.

Library of Congress Cataloging-in-Publication Data
A CIP catalog record for this book has been applied for at the Library of Congress.

This book was prepared in particular as part of the activity at the Interdisciplinary Center for Research on Deradicalization of the Jan Długosz University in Częstochowa.

The Publication is funded by Jan Dlugosz University in Czestochowa.

Cover illustration: Courtesy of Benjamin Ben Chaim.

ISSN 2191-3250
ISBN 978-3-631-90258-5 (Print)
E-ISBN 978-3-631-90830-3 (E-Book)
E-ISBN 978-3-631-90831-0 (E-PUB)
DOI 10.3726/b21166

Published by Peter Lang GmbH, Berlin, Deutschland

info@peterlang.com - www.peterlang.com

This publication has been peer reviewed.

Contents

Preface

We present to you a monograph titled "Formalized Access to Free Pre-litigation Legal Aid. Analysis Based on Examples of Ukraine, Poland, Great Britain and Sweden". This study is the result of several years of research conducted at the Faculty of Law and Economics of Jan Długosz University in Częstochowa. The outcome of this work is the formulation of practical *de lege lata* and *de lege ferenda* conclusions.

The authors of the monograph endeavoured to present legal solutions in the field of free pre-litigation legal aid from a comparative perspective, taking into account, on the one hand, the theoretical and legal basis for the functioning of free pre-litigation legal aid, and on the other hand, the practical aspects of its implementation using the example of the following countries:

1. Kingdom of Sweden (as an example of a country with a formed democracy and immense legislative experience in the field);
2. The Republic of Ukraine (as an example of an "emerging democracy");
3. The United Kingdom of Great Britain and Northern Ireland (as an example of a country with a *common law* system and formed democracy); and
4. The Republic of Poland.

This approach made it possible to illustrate the problems related to the provision of free legal assistance before the court and to show that the issues discussed are important from a theoretical point of view on the one hand, and of great practical importance on the other. The argument in favour of the choice of particular problems was their social significance and usefulness.

The monograph concerns solutions adopted in mentioned countries as of 2 June 2023. The work includes the content of the expert opinions prepared at the request of the Institute of Justice:

(a) B. Przywora, A. Wróbel, Analiza prawnoporównawcza sposobów finansowania oraz metod weryfikacji jakości systemu pomocy prawnej i poradnictwa obywatelskiego na tle wybranych państw europejskich, Warsaw 2022.
(b) B. Przywora, A. Wróbel, Poradnictwo obywatelskie w świetle badań prawnoporównawczych, Warsaw 2020.

We hope that the presented monograph will allow readers to deepen their knowledge of free legal aid from a standpoint of comparative law, contributing to further discussions in the field. The work can be a valuable source of knowledge for students, researchers and practitioners participating in legislative processes.

Editors

Introduction

One of the constitutional obligations of states is the protection of the individual (defence of human rights).[1] This is a positive obligation[2] and involves a commitment on the part of the state to protect the weaker individual.[3] Such state activities include the social welfare system, which includes free pre-litigation legal aid covering various forms (including civic counselling and legal education).

The authors attempted to present legal solutions in the field of unpaid pre-litigation legal aid in comparative terms, taking into account, on the one hand, the theoretical and legal basis for the functioning of free pre-litigation legal aid, and on the other hand, the practical aspects of its implementation using the example of the following countries:

1. The Kingdom of Sweden (as an example of a country with a formed democracy);
2. The Republic of Ukraine (as an example of an "emerging democracy");
3. The United Kingdom of Great Britain and Northern Ireland (as an example of a country with a *common law* system); and
4. The Republic of Poland.

On the one hand, the analysis of Swedish solutions is supported by their "maturity", since the system is well established internationally. It is an interesting

1 Jan Paweł II, *Nauczanie społeczne*, t. 3, Warszawa 1984, p. 165; see also: Human Rights. New Dimensions and Challenges Edited By J. Symonides, Routledge 1998

2 More C. Mik, *Teoria obowiązków pozytywnych państw-stron traktatów w dziedzinie praw człowieka na przykładzie Europejskiej Konwencji Praw Człowieka*, [in:] *Księga Jubileuszowa Profesora Tadeusza Jasudowicza*, red. J. Białocerkiewicz, M. Balcerzak, A. Czeczko-Durlak, Toruń 2004, pp. 257–276; see also: E. H. Morawska, *Zobowiązania pozytywne państw-stron Konwencji o ochronie praw człowieka i podstawowych wolności*, Warszawa 2016.

3 See also: I. Lipowicz, *O mądre prawo i wrażliwe państwo*, Warszawa 2013, pp. 314–315; M. Florczak-Wątor, *Podstawy prawne obowiązków ochronnych państwa w Konstytucji RP*, [in:] *Ochrona praw człowieka. Zagadnienia praktyczne*, red. A. Hauser, M. Urbaniak, Poznań 2019, p. 41; J. Czepek, *Zobowiązania pozytywne państwa w sferze praw człowieka pierwszej generacji na tle Europejskiej Konwencji Praw Człowieka*, Olsztyn 2014, pp. 21–26; S. Nitecki, *Solidarność a pomoc społeczna*, [in:] *Państwo solidarne*, red. A. Łabno, Warszawa 2018, p. 186; see also: M. Florczak-Wątor, *Horyzontalny wymiar praw konstytucyjnych*, Kraków 2014.

example of a legal aid system created as a result of evolution. The Swedish legal system is quite peculiar, as it provides for a very broadly defined institution of legal aid in the form of legal advice, legal assistance and legal aid under the rules governing criminal and civil proceedings. The Swedish legislator has abandoned the concept of free counselling in favour of a system of cost participation by the party. Reaching for Swedish solutions is justified bearing in mind the originality of the system on the one hand, and on the other hand the search in Poland for an optimal model of free pre-litigation legal aid.

We took a special approach in the analysis of Ukrainian norms, which is justified given the political situation in eastern Europe, and consequently the need to guarantee legal protection for individuals, especially mothers fleeing with their children.

Finally, the rationale behind the analysis of the legal aid and citizens' advice system in the United Kingdom of Great Britain and Northern Ireland is that it is one of the pre-eminent and exemplary systems in the world. The United Kingdom has a system of legal assistance or legal representation called "legal aid". The designed solutions are intended to provide assistance to low-income people to ensure the realisation of the individual's rights to a fair trial.[4] The peculiarity of this system is the commissioning of tasks to NGOs and the provision of funds to carry out this task through grants.

Such extensive comparative research has not yet been conducted in Poland. Nor has a similarly framed research problem yet been undertaken in the Polish literature. In order to illustrate the relevance of the issue of free legal aid in general, the work refers to international law, the law of the European Union and the legislation of the Council of Europe. The question arises: how, in the light of these norms, is free pre-litigation legal aid understood and what elements make up this concept? Such a problem is important in view of the fact that in addition to the institution of free legal aid one can see other constructions (e.g. in Poland, free civic counselling). In the context of the discussed issue, it is important to establish minimum standards for legal aid.[5] Taking into account: (a) international; (b) European Union; and (c) Council of Europe standards is important

---

4 See also: https://e-justice.europa.eu/content_fundamental_rights-176-ew-pl.do?member=1 (access: 03.12.2022).

5 In the literature, see e.g.: S. Trociuk, *Pomoc prawna dla osób ubogich jako forma zapewnienia skutecznego dostępu do krajowego i europejskiego wymiaru sprawiedliwości*, [in:] *Dostęp obywateli do europejskiego wymiaru sprawiedliwości*, red. H. Izdebski, H. Machińska, Warszawa 2005, p. 142.

for the implementation of Article 9 of the Constitution of the Republic of Poland of 2 April 1997,[6] from which it follows that Poland complies with international law binding on it (e.g. the standards of the Council of Europe in the field of democracy, rule of law and in the area of protection of human rights[7]). Poland, by ratifying international agreements, undertook to respect the rights arising from them; in particular, the European Convention on Human Rights[8] (ECHR) as an international agreement is part of the national legal order and is subject to direct application by all public authorities with precedence over domestic laws.[9] The question arises to what extent international and European law influence national legislation on the institution of free pre-litigation legal aid, and to what extent they impact other forms of assistance provided by states (e.g. civic counselling, mediation or legal education). Providing an answer to the question posed in this way is important in the context of seeking a legal basis for the construction of a system of free pre-litigation legal aid covering various forms of assistance (including civic counselling, mediation or legal education).

The analysis uses reports prepared for the Institute of Justice on the legal basis for the creation of forms of civil counselling in the light of international documents and the legislation of selected countries.[10] The study reached beyond the

---

6 Dz.U. Nr 78, poz. 483 ze zm.

7 More: J. Jaskiernia, *Rada Europy jako organizacja międzynarodowa kreująca i oddziaływująca na implementację standardów demokratycznych*, [in:] *Rada Europy a przemiany demokratyczne w państwach Europy Środkowej i Wschodniej w latach 1989–2009*, red. J. Jaskiernia, Warszawa 2010; see also: P. Sarnecki, *Komentarz do art. 9 Konstytucji RP*, [in:] *Konstytucja Rzeczypospolitej Polskiej. Komentarz*, t. 1, red. L. Garlicki, M. Zubik, Warszawa 2016. B. Banaszak, *Prawo konstytucyjne*, Warszawa 2015, pp. 134–136; K. Wójtowicz, *Komentarz do art. 9 Konstytucji RP*, [in:] *Konstytucja RP*, t. 1, *Komentarz do art. 1–86*, red. M. Safjan, L. Bosek, Warszawa 2016; see also judgment of the Constitutional Court from 27.04. 2005 r., P 1/05, OTK-A 2005, nr 4, poz. 42; judgment of the Constitutional Court from 11.05. 2005 r., K 18/04, OTK-A 2005, nr 5, poz. 49.

8 Dz.U. z 1993 r. Nr 61, poz. 284 ze zm.

9 Compare: L. Garlicki, *Rola sędziego krajowego w procesie wykonywania orzeczeń Europejskiego Trybunału Praw Człowieka*, [in:] *IX Seminarium Warszawskie. Dysfunkcje polskiego prawa – jak poprawić system środków prawnych w Polsce?*, Warszawa 2016, p. 36; source: https://www.gov.pl/web/dyplomacja/seminaria-warszawskie-publikacje (access: 12.11.2022).

10 B. Przywora, A. Wróbel, *Analiza prawnoporównawcza sposobów finansowania oraz metod weryfikacji jakości systemu pomocy prawnej i poradnictwa obywatelskiego na tle wybranych państw europejskich*, Warszawa 2022; B. Przywora, A. Wróbel, *Poradnictwo obywatelskie w świetle badań prawnoporównawczych*, Warszawa 2020.

discussion of theoretical issues to the practice of functioning of free legal aid in the countries analysed. This required an analysis of Swedish, Ukrainian, British and Polish sources. The book takes into account the issue of functioning during the COVID-19 pandemic and the related order to limit direct contacts, which was particularly important in the context of an individual's access to free legal aid in its various forms. Although various world-wide technological solutions have been indicated, facilitating such contacts, direct interactions cannot be entirely replaced by them, and the results achieved are varied.[11]

11 J. Winczorek, *Pandemia COVID-19 a dostęp do prawa. Polska na tle wyników badania międzynarodowego*, „Państwo i Prawo" 2020, nr 12, p. 39; see also the literature cited there: M. Velicogna, E. Steigenga, S. Taal, A. Schmidt, *Connecting EU jurisdictions: Exploring how to open justice across member states through ICT*, "Social Science Computer Review" 2008; M. Barendrecht, *Rechtwijzer: Why Online Supported Dispute Resolution Is Hard to Implement*, International Legal Aid Group Conference, 14–16.06.2017; O. Rabinovich-Einy, E. Katsh, *Access to digital justice: Fair and efficient processes for the Modern Age*, "Cardozo Journal of Conflict Resolution" 2016, nr 16, pp. 637–657; M. Araszkiewicz, *Technologie informacyjne a nieodpłatna pomoc prawna*, Warszawa 2015, p. 71; B. R. Hough, *Let's not make it worse. Issues to consider in adopting new technology*, "Harvard Journal of Law & Technology" 2012, nr 26, pp. 256–266; L. Rexer, P. Malone, *Overcoming barriers to adoption of effective technology strategies for improving access to justice*, "Harvard Journal of Law & Technology" 2012, nr 26, pp. 305–324; A. D. Reiling, *Technology for Justice: How Information Technology Can Support Judicial Reform*, Leiden 2009; also see: A. Chavan, *Mobile strategies for legal services*, "Harvard Journal of Law & Technology" 2012, nr 26, pp. 267–278.

Research methods

Several research methods were required in the execution of the study's subject matter. Due to the specificity of the study, in particular, the *legal-dogmatic method* was used, making it possible to determine both the intention of the legislator and the content of legal norms (the Constitution of the Republic of Poland, international acts and other domestic acts), as well as reports and information on the provision of free legal aid.

In order to present the institution of free legal aid in comparative terms, *the comparative legal research method was used.* This made it possible to highlight the broader perspective of the considerations undertaken. The comparative legal research method[1] is divided into several stages. Stage one consists of formulating the problem by posing a specific question or appropriate research hypothesis. Stage two is the selection of the material to be compared. Most often, appropriate systems are selected that are suitable for comparison because of cultural similarities, the individuality of the solutions they contain and their practical significance. The third stage involves the study of fragments of the selected legal systems without providing evaluations. After sufficient description, the comparatist evaluates the studied institutions by showing similarities, differences and identical elements. The penultimate stage consists of building a system of comparative results, which can be presented, for example, by borrowing solutions adopted in the countries under comparison. The last stage consists in critically evaluating the information obtained from the comparison. Konrad Zweigert and Hein Kötz promote the functionalist approach, saying that at its core is an attempt to find legal institutions or norms that play an appropriate social role.[2]

The authors chose the solutions adopted in Ukraine, in the Kingdom of Sweden and in Great Britain and Northern Ireland. Even a cursory analysis gives grounds for concluding that the Ukrainian legal aid system is one of the most extensive legal aid (including primary legal aid) provisions of civic guidance. It is also characteristic that this system also has an extensive system of quality control of the legal aid system. Thus, the inclusion of Ukrainian solutions is justified on the one hand by the fact that they are relatively new, and on the other by the

1 K. Zweigert, H. Kötz, *Introduction to Comparative Law*, New York 1998, p. 15.
2 Zweigert and Kötz, *Introduction*, p. 15.

political situation in which Ukrainian society has found itself in connection with the armed conflict on the part of Russia.

The choice of the second system analysed – that of Sweden – was determined by the fact that it is one of the most mature among the European systems of legal aid (including civil counselling), being the result of a long evolution. On the other hand, we justified the inclusion of the solutions of the United Kingdom of Great Britain and Northern Ireland as an example of a country with a *common law* system.

To a certain extent, *the legal-historical method* was also used, allowing us to discuss the process of formation of statutory norms on the regulation of free legal aid.

Also used was a method of institutional analysis, that is, a method for researching the broader sources of law, extending the traditional approach to the study of law with elements that allow empirical knowledge of the reasons for the creation of specific legal norms and the socio-economic effects of their functioning.[3]

The study also used the results of an audit conducted by the Supreme Audit Office[4] and tabular data on the provision of free legal aid, obtained from the Ministry of Justice and the Ombudsman, as well as opinions on the amendment of the law on free legal aid,[5] case law (especially of the Constitutional Tribunal

3 The institutional approach to research on the sources of law is used in research conducted by „Stowarzyszenie Badań nad Źródłami i Funkcjami Prawa", see also P. Chmielnicki, *Metodyka badań nad materialnymi źródłami prawa. Cz. 1. Podstawy*, „PrzPrPub" 2012, nr 3, pp. 90–101; *Metodyka badań nad materialnymi źródłami prawa. Cz. 2. Uzasadnienie i objaśnienia poszczególnych faz badań*, „PrzPrPubl" 2012, nr 4, pp. 72–101; *Pochodzenie, tworzenie i efektywność prawa*, Warszawa 2014.

4 Informacja o wynikach kontroli. Funkcjonowanie systemu nieodpłatnej pomocy prawnej 2018, LOP 430.001.2018, Nr ew. 4/2018/P/17/090/LOP, dostęp: https://www.nik.gov.pl/plik/id,16874,vp,19432.pdf (dostęp: 6 grudnia 2021 r.) – dalej: Informacja NIK.

5 Np. J. Waszczuk-Napiórkowska, *Opinia prawna dotycząca projektu ustawy o nieodpłatnej pomocy prawnej, nieodpłatnej informacji prawnej oraz edukacji prawnej społeczeństwa* (druk nr 3338), Warszawa, 25 maja 2015 r., Biuro Analiz Sejmowych Kancelaria Sejmu, http://orka.sejm.gov.pl/rexdomk7.nsf/Opdodr?OpenPage&nr=3338 (dostęp: 24 czerwca 2022 r.); K. Konieczko, *Opinia do ustawy o nieodpłatnej pomocy prawnej oraz edukacji prawnej (druk nr 962)*, Kancelaria Senatu, Biuro Legislacyjne, 9 lipca 2015 r., https://www.senat.gov.pl/gfx/senat/userfiles/_public/k8/dokumenty/opinie/079/o/962.pdf (dostęp: 24 czerwca 2022 r.); K. Konieczko, *Opinia do ustawy o zmianie ustawy o nieodpłatnej pomocy prawnej oraz edukacji prawnej oraz niektórych innych ustaw (druk nr 865)*, 26 czerwca 2018 r., Kancelaria Senatu, Biuro Legislacyjne, https://www.senat.gov.pl/gfx/senat/pl/senatekspertyzy/4743/plik/865o.pdf (dostęp: 24 czerwca 2022 r.).

and administrative courts) and other studies.[6] The functioning of the system of free legal aid (for a certain period of time) in the state of epidemic due to SARS-CoV-2 virus infections[7] was also taken into account. This significantly affected the functioning of the system of free legal aid. The analysis included solutions to

6 A. Peisert, T. Schimanek, A. Winiarska, M. Waszak (ed.), *Poradnictwo prawne i obywatelskie w Polsce: stan obecny i wizje przyszłości*, Warszawa 2013; see also: J. Winczorek, *Dostęp do poradnictwa. Stan obecny i możliwości zmiany*, [in:] *Poradnictwo prawne i obywatelskie – system, koszty, innowacje*, red. G. Wiaderek, Warszawa 2014; A. Zoll, *Dostęp do informacji prawnej jako prawo obywatelskie*, [in:], *Informacja prawna a prawa obywatela. Konferencja z okazji XXXV-lecia informatyki prawniczej w Polsce i XV-lecia Systemu Informacji Prawnej LEX, Gdańsk, 19–20 czerwca 2006*, red. K. Grajewski, J. Warylewski, Warszawa 2006; B. Przywora, *Normatywny model przedsądowej nieodpłatnej pomocy prawnej w Polsce*, Warszawa 2019; B. Przywora, A. Wróbel, *Poradnictwo obywatelskie w świetle badań prawnoporównawczych*, Warszawa 2020, https://iws.gov.pl/wp-content/uploads/2021/01/IWS_Przywora-B.-Wróbel-A._Poradnictwo-obywatelskie-w-świetle-badań-prawnoporównawczych.pdf (access: 24.06.2022).; zob. także: G. Wiaderek [in:] *System nieodpłatnego poradnictwa prawnego i obywatelskiego w Polsce. Propozycje rozwiązań modelowych i założeń polityki państwa*, Warszawa 2013, https://www.ekonomiaspoleczna.gov.pl/download/files/PPIO/System-nieodplatnego-ppio-w-polsce.pdf (access: 24.06.2022 r.); A. Witkowska, *Przegląd przepisów zawierających odniesienia dotyczące poradnictwa prawnego i obywatelskiego*, Warszawa 2012, https://www.inpris.pl/fileadmin/user_upload/documents/pomoc_prawna/PrzeglÄ...d_przepisÅłw_zawierajÄ...cych_odniesienia_dotyczÄ...ce_pomocy_prawnej_i_obywatelskiej.pdf (access: 24.06.2022); G. Wiaderek (ed.), *Poradnictwo prawne i obywatelskie – system, koszty, innowacje*, Warszawa 2014, https://www.academia.edu/8085878/Poradnictwo_prawne_i_obywatelskie_system_koszty_innowacje (access: 24.06.2022); A. S. Bartnik, K. J. Kowalska, *Nieodpłatna pomoc prawna*, Warszawa 2019; J. Wegner, B. Wróblewski, *Prawo jednostki do nieodpłatnej pomocy prawnej*, „PPP" 2021, nr 6, pp. 5–18; D. Daniluk, *Świadczenie nieodpłatnego poradnictwa obywatelskiego przez radcę prawnego lub adwokata a obowiązek zachowania tajemnicy zawodowej i unikania konfliktu interesów*, „Radca Prawny ZN" 2022, nr 1, pp. 29–40; D. Daniluk, Nieodpłatne poradnictwo *obywatelskie w świetle ustawy o nieodpłatnej pomocy prawnej, nieodpłatnym poradnictwie obywatelskim oraz edukacji prawnej. Wymiar teoretyczny i praktyczny*, „PPP" 2022, nr 10, pp. 41–56.

7 Zob. rozporządzenie Ministra Zdrowia z 20 marca 2020 r. w sprawie ogłoszenia na obszarze Rzeczypospolitej Polskiej stanu epidemii (Dz.U. poz. 491 ze zm.; tekst jedn. Dz.U. z 2022 r. poz. 340); uchylone.

adapt the system of free pre-litigation legal aid to the changed social reality and ensure the availability of services.[8]

Such an approach has consequently made it possible to assess the application of norms on free legal aid (covering various forms, including citizens' advice, mediation and legal education) and to identify conclusions, including *de lege ferenda* postulates.

8 Ocena Ministra Sprawiedliwości z realizacji zadań z zakresu nieodpłatnej pomocy prawnej, nieodpłatnego poradnictwa obywatelskiego oraz edukacji prawnej za 2021 rok.

Chapter I. Free pre-litigation legal aid – analysis from the perspective of international and European law

1.1. Preliminary remarks

The purpose of this chapter was to synthetically introduce the reader to the legal basis under international and European law on free legal aid at the pre-litigation stage. The question arises whether and, if so then, to what extent international and European law influence the legislation of countries in the field of free legal aid at the pre-litigation stage (including also: civic counselling, mediation or legal education).[1] Addressing this issue is important, given the situation that, in the last few decades, the issue of equalising opportunities for the vulnerable individual and realising the principle of social justice has gained particular importance and many regulations have been enacted, especially regarding access to justice.[2]

1.2. United Nations system

First of all, it is reasonable to point to the regulations of the universal declaration of human rights of 10 December 1948.[3] Although much scholarly reflection has

1 The study uses the database of sources of international law, the Council of Europe and the European Union contained in the work: B. Przywora, *Normatywny model przedsądowej nieodpłatnej pomocy prawnej w Polsce*, Warszawa 2019.

2 More: A. Ploszka, *Publicznoprawny status jednostki skrajnie ubogiej*, Warszawa 2019, p. 19; on the concept of the administration of justice, see also: J. Nowacki, *Sprawiedliwość legalna a „wymiar sprawiedliwości"*, [in:] *Współczesne problemy procesu karnego i wymiaru sprawiedliwości. Księga ku czci Profesora Kazimierza Marszała*, red. P. Hofmański, K. Zgryzek, Katowice 2003, pp. 300–313.

3 Text available at: http://libr.sejm.gov.pl/tek01/txt/onz/1948.html (access: 21.11.2020); see also: Emerging Areas of Human Rights in the 21 st Century. The Role of the Universal Declaration of Human Rights, edited By M. Odello, S. Cavandoli, Routledge 2011; Contemporary Human Rights ChallengesThe Universal Declaration of Human Rights and its Continuing RelevanceEdited by C. Ferstman, A. Goldberg, T. Gray, L. Ison, R. Nathan and M. Newman, Routledge 2018; The Universal Declaration of Human Rights: fifty years and Beyond, Edited by Y. Danieli, E. Stamatopoulou C. Dias, Routledge 2018

already been devoted to it,[4] it is the starting point for an analysis of issues in the area of human rights. Although the universal declaration of human rights is not of a binding nature (it is a resolution of the general assembly of the UN), nonetheless its norms began the process of codification and development of international human rights standards and the system of legal protection. In this regard, the right to a court of law, which is a guarantee for the protection of human rights, is of key importance.[5] It results in obligations (moral as well as political) for UN member states.[6] In light of its provisions, everyone is also equal before the law and has the right to legal protection without discrimination of any kind (Article 7). Everyone also has the right to effective appeal to competent national courts against acts that violate fundamental rights granted by the Constitution or laws (Article 8). Moreover, according to Article 10 of the Universal Declaration of Human Rights, everyone has the right, under conditions of full equality, to have his or her case fairly and publicly heard by an independent and impartial tribunal, which will decide on his or her rights and obligations or the validity of any criminal charge against him or her. To some extent, Article 11 of the Universal Declaration of Human Rights can also provide such a basis for building a system of free legal aid, for it stipulates that anyone accused of a criminal act enjoys the presumption of innocence until his guilt is lawfully proven in a public trial, during which he enjoys all the guarantees necessary for his defence. It is also worth taking into consideration Article 14 of the Universal Declaration of Human Rights, from which stems the right to seek and enjoy asylum in another country in the event of persecution. However, this right cannot be invoked in the case of a prosecution initiated for the commission of a common (non-political)

---

4 See also: D. Całkiewicz, A. Rotkiewicz, *Prawo pomocy jako gwarancja prawa do sądu dla najuboższych w świetle prawa międzynarodowego i unijnego oraz w przepisach ustawy – Prawo o postępowaniu sądowoadministracyjnym*, [in:] *Dziesięć lat polskich doświadczeń w Unii Europejskiej. Problemy prawnoadministracyjne*, red. J. Sługocki, t. 2, Warszawa 2014, p. 541; P. Przybysz, *Prawo do sądu w sprawach administracyjnych*, [in:] *Prawo administracyjne w okresie transformacji ustrojowej*, red. E. Knosala, A. Matan, G. Łaszczyca, Kraków 1999, p. 350; J. Symonides, *Powszechna Deklaracja Praw Człowieka (po 60 latach od jej przyjęcia)*, „Państwo i Prawo" 2008, nr 12, p. 11; B. Przywora, *Free legal assistance as an instrument in protecting the right of foreigners in the Republic of Poland – a contributions to the discussion*, „Annuals of The Administration and Law" 2020, nr XX(1), p. 31.

5 See also: J. Gołaczyński, A. Krzywonos, *Prawo do sądu*, [in:] *Prawa i wolności obywatelskie w Konstytucji RP*, red. B. Banaszak, A. Preisner, Warszawa 2002, p. 732.

6 M. Granat, *Prawo konstytucyjne. Pytania i odpowiedzi*, Warszawa 2019, p. 119.

crime or an act contrary to the purposes and principles of the United Nations.[7] Although the indicated norms do not directly define the institution of free pre-litigation legal aid (or civic counselling), they do, however, indirectly allow it to be derived in order to ensure due process of law.

Legal aid in a broad sense (including at the pre-litigation stage), understood in terms of informing the refugee of their rights and obligations, can provide important assistance to those with refugee status.[8] Thus, attention should be paid to Article 16 of the Convention Relating to the Status of Refugees[9] (drawn up in Geneva on 28 July 1951).[10] From this provision stems the right of a refugee to free access to the courts in the territories of all contracting States (paragraph 1), especially since the Convention explicitly emphasises the refugee's status in the country of permanent residence. A refugee should be treated as a citizen of the state in terms of access to courts or legal aid (paragraph 2). Article 25 of the Convention should also be emphasised, under which:

> If the exercise of a right by a refugee would ordinarily require the assistance of the authorities of a foreign State to which he cannot apply, the Contracting State on whose territory he is habitually resident shall cause such assistance to be obtained either from its own authorities or from some international body. (paragraph 1)

In the context of the issue at hand one should take into account the provisions of the International Covenant on Civil and Political Rights[11]. This shows that each state that is party to the Covenant has undertaken to respect the rights recognised therein and to guarantee those rights to persons within its territory and subject to its jurisdiction, regardless of any differences (e.g. race, colour, sex,

---

7 See also: K. Motyka, *Prawa człowieka. Wprowadzenie. Wybór źródeł*, Lublin 2004, p. 127.

8 See also: R. Wieruszewski, P. Stupak, *Postępowanie o nadanie statusu uchodźcy w Polsce*, [in:] *Ochrona praw człowieka. Zagadnienia praktyczne*, red. A. Hauser, M. Urbaniak, Poznań 2019, p. 243.

9 Dz.U. z 1991 r. Nr 119, poz. 515.

10 Zob. także: Przywora, *Free*, p. 33.

11 Dz.U. z 1977 r. Nr 38, poz. 167; See also: R. Wieruszewski (ed.), *Międzynarodowy Pakt Praw Obywatelskich (Osobistych) i Politycznych. Komentarz*, Warszawa 2012; S. Joseph, M. Castan, *The International Covenant on Civil and Political Rights: Cases, Materials*, Oxford University Press 2013; Ch. Tomuschat, *International Covenant on Civil and Political Rights*, United Nations Audiovisual Library of International Law (access: https://legal.un.org/avl/pdf/ha/iccpr/iccpr_e.pdf, 18.07.2023); D. McGoldrick, *The Human Rights Committee. Its Role in the Development of the International Covenant on Civil and Political Rights*, 2nd edition, Clarendon Press, Oxford 1994.

language, religion, political or other opinion, or national origin) (Article 2(1) of the ICCPR) and to take appropriate measures to introduce legislative or other measures to ensure the realisation of those rights under the Covenant (Article 2(2) of the ICCPR). States have undertaken to ensure:

(a) everyone an effective remedy for violations of freedoms or rights under the Covenant;
(b) that the right of everyone to a remedy is determined by the competent judicial, administrative or legislative authorities, or by any other competent authority provided for in the legal system of a given state, and the development of instruments of judicial protection; and
(c) implementation of legal remedies by the competent authorities (Article 2(3) of the ICCPR).[12]

Article 14 of the ICCPR[13] should also be emphasised, from which it follows that all people are equal before courts and tribunals, and everyone has the right to a fair and public hearing by a competent, independent and impartial tribunal, established by law, in deciding on the merits of the charge against him in criminal cases or on his rights and obligations in civil cases (paragraph 1).[14] Hence, a person accused of a crime has the right, on an equal basis, to, among other things, adequate time and opportunity to prepare his defence and to guarantee communication with counsel of his choice (Article 14(3)(b) of the ICCPR), to defend himself personally or through counsel of his choice. It is also important to ensure that the accused person is informed, if he or she does not have a

12 See also: L. Garlicki, K. Wojtyczek, *Komentarz do art. 77 Konstytucji RP*, [in:] *Konstytucja Rzeczypospolitej Polskiej. Komentarz*, red. L. Garlicki, M. Zubik, t. 2, Warszawa 2016, pp. 830–831.

13 The importance of Art. 14 ICCPR also draws attention to, among others: General Comment No. 32: Article 14: Right to Equality before Courts and Tribunals and to Fair Trial, CCPR/C/GC/32, source: https://tbinternet.ohchr.org/_layouts/15/treatybodyexternal/Download.aspx?symbolno=CCPR%2FC%2FGC%2F32&Lang=en access: 24.07.2023; A. Bisztyga – see: A. Bisztyga, *Prawo do rozpatrzenia sprawy w rozsądnym terminie. Nowe działania: ADR, e-sąd*, [in:] *Transformacja systemów wymiaru sprawiedliwości w państwach Europy Środkowej i wschodniej w latach 1990–2010*, red. J. Jaskiernia, Toruń 2011, p. 751; see also: Z. Czeszejko-Sochacki, *Prawo do sądu w świetle Konstytucji Rzeczypospolitej Polskiej (ogólna charakterystyka)*, „Państwo i Prawo" 1997, nr 11–12, pp. 90, 92–93;

14 Compare: Gołaczyński and Krzywonos, *Prawo*, p. 735; Całkiewicz and Rotkiewicz, *Prawo*, s. 541.

defence counsel, of the existence of the above right and to have a defence counsel appointed for him or her whenever the interests of justice so require, without incurring defence costs when the accused does not have sufficient means to pay for them (Article 14(3)(d) of the ICCPR). It is important that the right to a trial is not illusory (apparent).[15]

The provisions of the International Covenant on Economic, Social and Cultural Rights[16] on social security (Article 9) should also be noted. The state's provision of free access to free pre-litigation legal aid is part of the realisation of the Covenant, that is, to give "the widest possible protection and assistance to the family as the natural and fundamental cell of society, particularly at its establishment and during the period of the family's responsibility for the care and upbringing of dependent children", to give special care to "the mother during a reasonable period before and after the birth of her child" and to take special steps "to ensure the protection and assistance of all children and adolescents without any discrimination based on origin or other grounds" (Article 10). The Covenant also guarantees the protection of children and adolescents "from economic and social exploitation" (Article 10).

The regulations of the Convention on the Elimination of All Forms of Discrimination against Women[17] are also relevant in this context. In the Convention, states undertook to take measures in all fields to ensure the full development and advancement of women and to ensure that they possess and exercise their human rights and fundamental freedoms on an equal basis with men (Article 3).

In addition, the provisions of the Convention on the Rights of the Child[18] (adopted by the United Nations General Assembly on 20 November 1989) are

---

15 A. Witkowska, *Przegląd przepisów zawierających odniesienia dotyczące poradnictwa prawnego i obywatelskiego*, Warszawa 2012, p. 9; source: http://www.inpris.pl/fileadmin/user_upload/documents/pomoc_prawna/Przegl%C3%84%E2%80%A6d_przepis%C4%82%C5%82w_zawieraj%C3%84%E2%80%A6cych_odniesienia_dotycz%C3%84%E2%80%A6ce_pomocy_prawnej_i_obywatelskiej.pdf (access: 14.11.2020).

16 Dz.U. z 1977 r. Nr 38, poz. 169, see also: Z. Kędzia, A. Hernandez-Połczyńska (ed.), *Międzynarodowy Pakt Praw Gospodarczych, Socjalnych i Kulturalnych. Komentarz*, Warszawa 2018; B. Saul, D. Kinley, J. Mowbray, *The International Covenant on Economic, Social and Cultural Rights*, Oxford University Press 2018.

17 Dz.U. z 1982 r. Nr 10, poz. 71.

18 Implementation Handbook for the Convention on the Rights of the Child, UNICEF 2007; also: M. D.Ruck, D.P. Keating, E. M. Saewyc, F. Earls, A. Ben-Arieh, *The United Nations Convention on the Rights of the Child: Its Relevance forAdolescents, Journal of Research on Adolescence,* Volume 26, Issue 1, pp.16-29.

relevant. The Convention is an international agreement ratified by Poland.[19] Poland has also ratified two additional protocols to the Convention.[20] The Convention sets forth the basic principles recognised by the parties to the treaty. Free pre-litigation legal aid serves to protect the rights of children from threats. Hence, the Convention implies, in particular, the obligation to undertake activities for the protection of the child against all forms of physical or psychological violence, harm, neglect, ill-treatment or exploitation (including sexual abuse) of children under the care of the parent, legal guardian and other person having custody of the child. The Convention also provides for the provision of free legal assistance to a child who is temporarily or permanently deprived of his or her family environment or who, for reasons in his or her best interests, cannot remain in that environment (Article 20(1) of the Convention), protection and assistance to a child seeking refugee status or recognised as a refugee in the light of the relevant rules of international law or internal applicable procedure (Article 22 of the Convention), as well as an instrument to strengthen the protection of the rights of a child with disabilities (Article 23(2) of the Convention), to assist parents or others responsible for the child in his or her development (Article 27(3) of the Convention). Civic counselling can also be understood in terms of a system of free legal or psychological assistance. The importance of free pre-litigation legal aid is also in guaranteeing children deprived of their liberty the right to have immediate access to legal or other responsible assistance and the right to defend their rights before a court or other competent, independent and impartial authority and to demand a prompt decision thereon (Art. 37(d) of the Convention), or in the area of creating norms, procedures or institutions to protect minors: especially children suspected, accused or found guilty of violating criminal laws (Article 40(3) of the Convention).

The free legal assistance may also implement the provisions of the Convention against Torture and Other Cruel, Inhuman or Degrading Treatment or Punishment.[21] This applies to persons at risk of torture or legal assistance to persons who have already been subjected to torture. The Convention obliges states to take effective measures; in particular, it is important to take legislative initiatives,

---

19 Journal of Laws of 1991 No. 120, item 526 as amended.

20 Optional Protocol to the Convention on the Rights of the Child on the involvement of children in armed conflict, 25 May 2000 (Dz.U. z 2007 r. Nr 91, poz. 608) and Optional Protocol to the Convention on the Rights of the Child on the sale of children, child prostitution and child pornography, 25 May 2000 (Dz.U. z 2007 r. Nr 76, poz. 494).

21 Dz.U. z 1989 r. Nr 63, poz. 378.

as well as administrative and judicial actions to "prevent torture throughout the territory under its jurisdiction" (Article 2(1) of the Convention).

Sources for creating solutions for free pre-litigation legal aid are also provided by the Declaration on the Rights of Mentally Retarded Persons (adopted by the UN General Assembly on 20 December 1971) and the Convention on the Rights of Persons with Disabilities (drawn up in New York on 13 December 2006).[22] The Convention indicates the directions in which state activity should be focused, leaving to states the choice of measures in this regard.[23] Its goal remains "to promote, protect and ensure the full and equal enjoyment of all human rights and fundamental freedoms by all persons with disabilities and to promote respect for their inherent dignity" (Article 1 of the Convention). The Convention is based on several principles, including:

1. non-discrimination;
2. full and effective participation and inclusion in society; and
3. equality of opportunity and accessibility (Article 3 of the Convention).

It is the duty of the state to take measures to provide reasonable accommodation (Art. 5 of the Convention) in the form of appropriate legislative, administrative and other measures to implement the rights recognised in the Convention; to amend or repeal existing laws, regulations, customs and practices that discriminate against persons with disabilities; to include the requirement to protect and promote the human rights of persons with disabilities in every policy and programme of action; to refrain from acts or practices that are inconsistent with the present Convention; to take all measures to eliminate discrimination on the basis of disability by any person, organisation or private enterprise; to provide accessible information to persons with disabilities about mobility objects, devices and assistive technologies, as well as other forms of assistance, services and facilities (Art. 4(1)–(2) of the Convention). As part of the broad discretion to ensure the effectiveness of the protection of persons with disabilities, the legislator may introduce arrangements for free pre-litigation legal assistance, especially in the context of strengthening the protection of the rights of persons with disabilities, such as equal opportunities and equal remuneration for work of equal value, safe and hygienic working conditions, including protection against harassment and

22 Dz.U. z 2012 r. poz. 1169.

23 The Constitutional Court in the case of number K 37/13 referred to the importance of the provisions of the Convention on the Rights of Persons with Disabilities: judgment of the Constitutional Court from 8.06.2016 r., K 37/13, OTK-A 2016, poz. 28.

compensation for harm suffered, ensuring that persons with disabilities enjoy labour rights and the right to organise into trade unions, on an equal basis with others, or enabling persons with disabilities to have effective access to general specialised and vocational counselling programmes, job placement services, and vocational and continuing education and training (Article 27(1)(b, c, d) of the Convention). The state should adopt an appropriate policy (strategy of action) towards the construction of systemic solutions, taking into account both social welfare institutions and NGOs. In particular, conducting legal education should be considered important.

1.3. Council of Europe system

Within the framework of the Council of Europe system[24], the Convention for the Protection of Human Rights and Fundamental Freedoms[25] (drawn up in Rome on 4 November 1950) is of fundamental importance. In particular, it concerns the formation of standards of individual rights[26] and the provision of protection to individuals in horizontal relations by taking positive action (the state as a guarantor of individual rights[27]). First and foremost, it is important to emphasise Article 6 of the ECHR, from which the standards of due process and fair hearing

---

24 See Also: M. Bond, *The Council of Europe: Structure, History and Issues in European Politics*, Routledge 2012; S. Schmahl, M. Breuer, *The Council of Europe: Its Law and Policies*, Oxford University Press 2017.

25 See also:W. A. Schabas, *The European Convention on Human Rights: A Commentary*, Oxford University Press 2015; L. Garlicki, [in:] *Konwencja o Ochronie Praw Człowieka i Podstawowych Wolności*, t. 1, *Komentarz do artykułów* 1–18, red. L. Garlicki, Warszawa 2010; A. Bisztyga, *Europejska Konwencja Praw Człowieka a Karta Praw Podstawowych Unii Europejskiej – stan kompatybilności czy konkurencyjności?*, „Przegląd Prawa Konstytucyjnego" 2011, nr 3, p. 180; P. Kruszyński, *Zasada prawa do obrony w świetle orzecznictwa Europejskiego Trybunału Praw Człowieka w Strasburgu – zagadnienia wybrane*, [in:] *Gaudium in litteris est. Księga Jubileuszowa ofiarowana Pani Profesor Genowefie Rejman z okazji osiemdziesiątych urodzin*, Warszawa 2005; M. A. Nowicki, *Wokół Konwencji Europejskiej. Komentarz do Europejskiej Konwencji Praw Człowieka*, Warszawa 2017.

Compare: M. Florczak-Wątor, *Rola sądów i trybunałów w kształtowaniu koncepcji horyzontalnego działania praw jednostki*, [in:] *Sądy i trybunały wobec problemu horyzontalnego działania praw jednostki*, red. M. Florczak-Wątor, Kraków 2015, p. 13.

26 See also: Granat, *Prawo*, p. 120; J. Jaskiernia, *Funkcje Konstytucji RP w dobie integracji europejskiej i radykalnych przemian politycznych*, Toruń 2020, pp. 252–253.

27 See also Florczak-Wątor, *Rola*, p. 13.

are derived.[28] This provision is a general principle with a broad application (paragraph 1), and also sets out specific guarantees for criminal proceedings (paragraphs 2 and 3)[29] and the necessary features regarding the structure of justice and the conduct of proceedings.[30] In the following paragraphs of Article 6 ECHR grants the accused of a criminal act at least the right to:

1. promptly receive detailed information in a language he understands about the nature and cause of the accusation against him;
2. having adequate time and opportunity to prepare a defence;
3. defend himself in person or by a defence attorney appointed by him, and, if he does not have sufficient means to pay for his defence, to have free use of an ex officio appointed defence attorney when the interests of justice so require;
4. examine or cause the examination of prosecution witnesses and to demand the presence and examination of defence witnesses under the same conditions as prosecution witnesses; and
5. use the free assistance of an interpreter if he or she does not understand or speak the language used in court (paragraph 3).

Instruments within the framework of free pre-litigation legal aid can be an instrument that strengthens, in particular, the implementation of Article 6(3)(c)

---

28 See also: B. Rainey, P. McCormick, C. Ovey, *The European Convention on Human Rights*, 2021; C. Grabenwarter (ed.), *European Convention on Human Rights*, 2023; W. A. Schabas, *The European Convention on Human Rights: A Commentary*, 2015; Bisztyga, *Prawo*, p. 751; P. Sarnecki, *Komentarz do art. 45 Konstytucji RP*, [in:] *Konstytucja Rzeczypospolitej Polskiej. Komentarz*, t. 1, red. L. Garlicki, M. Zubik, Warszawa 2016, p. 241; see also: M. A. Nowicki, *Prawo do rzetelnego procesu sądowego*, [in:] *Europejski Trybunał Praw Człowieka. Wybór orzeczeń*, red. M. A. Nowicki, Warszawa 2013, pp. 151–171; Przywora, *Normatywny*, pp. 89–104.

29 See also: P. Czech, L. Heschl, K. Lukas, M. Nowak, & G. Oberleitner (eds), *European Yearbook on Human Rights*, 2019, pp. 295–312; Nikos Vogiatzis, *Interpreting the Right to Interpretation under Article 6(3)(e) ECHR: A Cautious Evolution in the Jurisprudence of the European Court of Human Rights?*, "Human Rights Law Review"; M. Wąsek-Wiaderek, *Prawo oskarżonego do posiadania obrońcy w świetle orzecznictwa Europejskiego Trybunału Praw Człowieka*, [in:] *Studia i analizy Sądu Najwyższego*, red. K. Ślebzak, t. 6, Warszawa 2012, pp. 331–360; P. Hofmański, A. Wróbel, *Komentarz do art. 6 EKPCz*, [in:] *Konwencja o Ochronie Praw Człowieka i Podstawowych Wolności. Komentarz do artykułów 1–18*, red. L. Garlicki, t. 1, Warszawa 2010, pp. 246–443.

30 Por. J. Podkowik, *Wymogi europejskiej Konwencji o ochronie praw człowieka i podstawowych wolności dotyczące sądownictwa wojskowego*, „Przegląd Sejmowy" 2010, nr 3(98), p. 86.

of the ECHR in ensuring the possession of a public defender even at the initial stage of criminal proceedings, by creating real access for persons without sufficient means to information about the conditions of access to legal aid and the possibility of benefiting from it.[31]

The Convention creates a so-called minimum standard for the rights of the accused[32] (i.e. trial of cases within a reasonable time[33] and the right to a free public defender when determined by the interests of justice and in the absence of adequate funds to pay defence costs).[34]

To some extent, the basis for the establishment of civic counselling can also be sought in Article 13 of the ECHR, from which stems the right to an effective remedy, and Article 14 of the ECHR, from which it follows that the enjoyment of the rights and freedoms enumerated in the Convention should be secured to the exclusion of discrimination based on such grounds as sex, race, colour, language, religion, political or other opinion, national or social origin, membership in a national minority, property, birth or any other ground.[35]

A positive obligation on the part of the state to construct an effective system of (legal) assistance for an effective right of access to court can be derived indirectly from Articles 6, 13 and 14 of the ECHR. At the same time, it is left to the states to choose the forms of action.[36] Free pre-litigation legal aid can be part of a system of assistance from the state, complementing other forms already in force in the assertion of rights.[37]

Other Council of Europe conventions should also be mentioned. In first place, the European Social Charter (drawn up on 18 October 1961).[38] This is important

31 Trociuk, *Pomoc*, p. 142; wyrok Wielkiej Izby Trybunału *w sprawie Salduz przeciwko Turcji* z 27 listopada 2008 r. (skarga nr 36391/02); Wąsek-Wiaderek, *Prawo*, p. 346.

32 W piśmiennictwie zob. np. Przybysz, *Prawo*, p. 350; see also: Całkiewicz and Rotkiewicz, *Prawo*, p. 542.

33 Szerzej: S. Waltoś, *Zasada w polskim procesie karnym*, [in:] *System Prawa Karnego Procesowego*, red. P. Hofmański, t. 3, cz. 1, *Zasady procesu karnego*, red. P. Wiliński, Warszawa 2014, p. 303; Mik, *Teoria*, p. 265.

34 See e.g. J. Barcik, T. Srogosz, *Prawo dostępu do adwokata w Polsce w świetle dyrektywy 2013/48/UE*, „Palestra" 2015, nr 7–8, p. 244.

35 More: M. A. Nowicki, *Komentarz do art. 14 EKPCz*, [in:] *Wokół Konwencji Europejskiej. Komentarz do Europejskiej Konwencji Praw Człowieka*, red. M. A. Nowicki, Warszawa 2017.

36 See also Flaga-Gieruszyńska, *Idea*, p. 55.

37 Compare Florczak-Wątor, *Horyzontalny*, pp. 33–43; Przywora, *Normatywny*, p. 103.

38 Dz.U. z 1999 r. Nr 8, poz. 67 ze zm.

for the protection of social rights,[39] including protection of employment and labour, social security, education, health, housing, legal and social protection. The European Social Charter commits to the effective protection of the rights of the worker; the establishment or maintenance of free employment services for all workers; the provision or promotion of both appropriate vocational guidance, training and vocational readaptation (Article 1 of the ECS) and, where necessary, the provision or promotion of services to assist persons (including persons with disabilities) in solving problems of career choice and advancement, taking into account individual aptitudes and the relationship of these aptitudes to employment opportunities. This type of assistance is to be free of charge. Various forms of free civic counselling can serve to make these norms a reality. All the more so since the European Social Charter implies the obligation of the state to create or maintain a social security system (Article 12 of the ECS). Through free pre-litigation legal aid, it remains possible to protect Article 15 of the ECS, that is, within the framework of taking the necessary measures to provide training facilities for persons with disabilities, including, if necessary, the establishment of specialised public or private institutions; specialised job placement services, facilitation of sheltered employment and measures to encourage employers to hire persons with disabilities), Article 16 (concerning social, legal and economic protection of the family) or Article 19 (in the area of protection of the rights of migrant workers and their families).

Attention should also be paid to the Convention on Action against Trafficking in Human Beings (drawn up in Warsaw on 16 May 2005, and ratified by Poland on 22 October 2008[40]). The goals of the Convention are, among others: to prevent and combat trafficking in human beings and to protect the human rights of trafficking victims, to establish a framework plan for the protection and assistance of victims and witnesses, with gender equality guaranteed, and to ensure effective investigation and prosecution (Article 1(1) of the Convention).

---

39 Jaskiernia, *Funkcje*, p. 253; on the European Social Charter see among others: B. Przywora, *Europejska Karta Społeczna jako wzorzec kontroli prawa w świetle orzecznictwa Trybunału Konstytucyjnego*, [in:] *Ochrona praw człowieka w Europie. Aksjologia, instytucje, nowe wyzwania, praktyka*, red. J. Jaskiernia, K. Spryszak, t. 3, Toruń 2017, pp. 202–211; see also: M. Wujczyk, *Europejski Komitet Praw Społecznych Rady Europy jako ponadpaństwowy organ ochrony praw człowieka*, [in:] *Instytucje ochrony praw człowieka*, red. B. Szmulik, A. Pogłodek, B. Przywora, Warszawa 2014; A. M. Świątkowski, *Karta Praw Społecznych Rady Europy*, Warszawa 2006; L. Samuel, *Fundamental Social Rights: Case-Law of the European Social Charter*, Strasbourg 2002.

40 Dz.U. z 2009 r. Nr 20, poz. 107.

With the help of free pre-litigation legal assistance, it is possible to promote the rights of victims (Article 3 of the Convention), and it can also be an instrument in the implementation of policies and programmes to prevent trafficking (e.g. through: research, information, awareness-raising and educational campaigns, social and economic initiatives, and training programmes aimed primarily at people at risk of becoming victims of trafficking, and anti-trafficking professionals) (Art. 5(2) of the Convention), as well as the taking of measures by parties to the Convention to enable legal migration, in particular through the dissemination of accurate information by relevant facilities, under conditions that allow legal entry and stay in its territory (Article 5(4) of the Convention), the creation of a protective environment for children (Article 5(5) of the Convention). The relevant actors in this regard are non-governmental organisations, other relevant organisations and civil society factors involved in the prevention of human trafficking and the protection and assistance of victims (Article 5(6) of the Convention). The Convention also implies an obligation to ensure that victims have access, from their first contact with the competent authorities, to information on relevant judicial and administrative proceedings in a language they understand, and to guarantee in domestic law the right of victims to obtain free legal assistance under the conditions laid down in its domestic law (Article 15 of the Convention). In implementing these regulations, various forms of free pre-litigation legal aid are important for persons who have experienced inhuman treatment in terms of their rights.

Also of note is the Council of Europe Convention on Preventing and Combating Violence against Women and Domestic Violence (done in Istanbul, 11 May 2011[41]). The Convention aims to:

1. protect women from all forms of violence and prevent, prosecute and eliminate violence against women and domestic violence;
2. contribute to the elimination of all forms of discrimination against women and to promote real equality between women and men, including by strengthening women's independent position;
3. create an overall framework, policy and action for the protection and support of all victims of violence against women and domestic violence;
4. support international cooperation to eliminate violence against women and domestic violence; and

41 Dz.U. z 2015 r. poz. 961

5. provide support and assistance to organisations and law enforcement agencies for effective cooperation to adopt an integrated approach to the elimination of violence against women and domestic violence (Article 1 of the Convention).

The Convention sets the direction of states' legislation. In particular, it obliges parties to introduce legislative and other measures and implement a nationwide effective, comprehensive and coordinated policy that includes all appropriate measures to prevent and combat the forms of violence covered by the Convention, and to ensure an holistic approach to violence against women (Article 7(1)). The implementation of these provisions may already take place at the stage of free pre-litigation legal assistance, to prevent forms of violence covered by this Convention committed by natural or legal persons (Article 12 (1) and (2)).

Additionally, mention should be made of the recommendations of the Committee of Ministers of the Council of Europe.[42] Their special role boils down to the development of a minimum catalogue of individual rights and freedoms, which should be ensured in all countries. The recommendations, although not legally binding, nevertheless influence the shape of legislation.[43] The recommendations of the Council of Europe are reflected in both European and Polish jurisprudence. In particular, it is worth noting the momentous importance of the explanatory memorandum to the ETHR judgment of 27 November 2008 in the case of Salduz *v.* Turkey, already cited in the work. In that judgment, the ETHR referred to a number of recommendations, including:

1. Recommendation of the Committee of Ministers to the Member States of the Council of Europe on New Ways of Dealing with Juvenile Delinquency and the Role of Juvenile Justice Authorities (Rec (2003)20), adopted on 24 September 2003;
2. minimum standards for the treatment of prisoners (Resolution (73) 5 of the Committee of Ministers of the Council of Europe); and
3. Recommendation of the Committee of Ministers to the Member States of the Council of Europe on European Prison Rules (Rec (2006/2)), adopted on 11

42 Przywora, *Normatywny*, pp. 129–133.

43 In the literature on soft law, see too: K. Spryszak, *Uniwersalne standardy z obszaru „miękkiego prawa"*, [in:] *Współczesne wyzwania państwa i prawa. Księga jubileuszowa z okazji 45-lecia pracy naukowej profesora Jerzego Jaskierni*, red. Ł. Baratyński, P. Ramiączek, K. Spryszak Toruń 2017, p. 371.

January 2006, indicating standards for all prisoners to have the right to legal counsel.

The Polish Supreme Court has also referred to the recommendations of the Committee of Ministers of the Council of Europe. For example, its resolution of 21 September 2000, III CZP 14/00,[44] referred, among other things, to international standards that have the character of soft international law, that is, Recommendation No. R(93)1 of 8 January 1993 of the Committee of Ministers of the Council of Europe to member states on effective access to law and justice for persons in situations of great poverty, which recommended that governments of member states take measures to facilitate access to law for such persons.[45]

The Constitutional Tribunal also referred to this recommendation (e.g. in the case P 4/04[46] regarding the constitutionality of the provisions of the Civil Code regarding the possibility of exemption from court costs in land and mortgage proceedings, the Constitutional Tribunal emphasised the importance of this recommendation relating to effective access to law and justice for the poorest). It is also worth noting the subsequent jurisprudence of the Constitutional Tribunal (e.g. the judgment of 25 November 2014 in the case K 54/13,[47] concerning the exclusion of the possibility of telephone communication between a temporarily detained person and defence counsel, the Constitutional Tribunal pointed to the recommendations contained in the Recommendation of the Committee of Ministers to the Member States of the Council of Europe on European Prison Rules (Rec(2006)2) and in the Directive of the European Parliament and of the Council 2013/48/EU of 22 October 2013 on the Right of Access to a Lawyer in Criminal Proceedings and European Arrest Warrant Proceedings and on the Right to Inform a Third Party of a Deprivation of Liberty and the Right to Communicate with Third Parties and Consular Authorities During Deprivation of Liberty[48]). In conclusion, although the recommendations of the Committee of the Council of Ministers cannot be attributed a binding character, they are relevant in the context of determining the direction of the organisation of the judiciary, in order to optimally implement the standards of the ECHR, the ICCPR or the CFR in particular (they influence the shape of national legislation, strengthening the

44 OSNC 2001, nr 2, poz. 21.

45 Zob. także Trociuk, *Pomoc*, p. 143.

46 Judgment of the Constitutional Court from 7.09. 2004 r., P 4/04, OTK-A 2004, nr 8, poz. 81.

47 OTK-A 2014, nr 10, poz. 114.

48 Dz.Urz. UE L 294, s. 1.

European process of harmonising human rights standards in terms of extending protection to the widest possible group of people).[49]

1.4. European Union regulations

The regulations of the European Union, especially the *Charter of Fundamental Rights of the European Union* (hereinafter *the Charter*),[50] are also important. With the entry into force of the Lisbon Treaty,[51] of which the Charter is an integral part, human rights have gained their rightful importance in the European Union. The relationship between the Charter of Fundamental Rights of the European Union and the Convention for the Protection of Human Rights and Fundamental Freedoms is defined by Article 6 (2) and (3) of the Treaty on European Union.[52] In the light of these regulations, the fundamental rights guaranteed by the Convention and arising from the constitutional traditions common to the Member States are part of European Union law, as general principles of law.[53] The Charter implies the prohibition of discrimination (Article 21(1) of the CFR).

---

49 Przywora, *Normatywny*, p. 133; O. Hałub, *Konstytucyjne gwarancje prawa do nieodpłatnej pomocy prawnej na etapie przedsądowym*, „Forum Prawnicze" 2016, nr 4, p. 73.

50 Wersja skonsolidowana Dz.Urz. UE C 202 z 2016 r, p. 389; See e.g. A. Wyrozumska, *Znaczenie prawne zmiany statusy Karty Praw Podstawowych Unii Europejskiej w Traktacie Lizbońskim oraz Protokołu polsko-brytyjskiego*, „Przegląd Sejmowy" 2008, nr 2(85), p. 26; B. Banaszak, *Zalety i wady Karty Praw Podstawowych Unii Europejskiej*, „Przegląd Sejmowy" 2008, nr 2(85), p. 10; zob. także: R. Wieruszewski, *Rola i znaczenie Karty Praw Podstawowych Unii Europejskiej dla ochrony praw człowieka*, „Przegląd Sejmowy" 2008, nr 2(85), p. 14; S. Biernat, *Czy Karta Praw Podstawowych Unii Europejskiej obowiązuje w Polsce?*, [in:] *Państwo prawa i prawo karne. Księga Jubileuszowa Profesora Andrzeja Zolla*, t. 1, red. P. Kardas, T. Sroka, W. Wróbel, Warszawa 2012; A. Wróbel (ed.), *Karta Praw Podstawowych Unii Europejskiej. Komentarz*, Warszawa 2020; A.J., Menéndez, Chartering Europe: Legal Status and Policy Implications of the Charter of Fundamental Rights of the European Union. JCMS: Journal of Common Market Studies, 2002 40: 471-490; J. Kokott, Ch. Sobbotta, *The Charter of Fundamental Rights of the European Union after Lisbon*, EUI AEL, 2010/06, Distinguished Lectures of the Academy; M.T. Gil-Bazo, The Charter of Fundamental Rights of the European Union and the Right to be Granted Asylum in the Union's Law, *Refugee Survey Quarterly*, Volume 27, Issue 3, 2008, Pages 33–52.

51 Traktat z Lizbony zmieniający Traktat o Unii Europejskiej i Traktat ustanawiający Wspólnotę Europejską z 13 grudnia 2007 r. (Dz.U. z 2009 r. Nr 203, poz. 1569).

52 Traktat o Unii Europejskiej (Dz. U. z 2004 r. Nr 90, poz. 864/30 ze zm.). See also: Granat, *Prawo*, p. 121.

53 See also: Bisztyga, *Europejska*, pp. 183–184.

Everyone also has the right to good administration, that is, to have his or her case dealt with impartially and fairly within a reasonable time by the institutions, bodies and agencies of the Union (Article 41(1) of the CFR), and the right to an effective remedy and access to an impartial court. Thus, the Charter mainly points to the so-called formal defence.[54] Article 48(2) of the CFR, which is significant in terms of guarantees concerning the right of defence, is also relevant. In these norms, the basis for the creation of forms of free pre-litigation legal aid should be sought. An effectively functioning system of assistance from the state can be considered in the context of the implementation of the standards of good administration.[55]

From the point of view of providing arguments for the construction of the institution of free pre-litigation legal aid, other acts should also be mentioned, in particular, Council Directive 2003/8/EC of 27 January 2003 to improve access to justice in cross-border disputes by establishing minimum common rules relating to legal aid in disputes of this nature.[56] Its purpose is to encourage the application for legal aid by persons without sufficient means when such aid is necessary to ensure effective access to justice and to guarantee an equal level of legal aid in cross-border disputes by establishing minimum common standards relating to legal aid.[57] In the light of this Directive, legal aid "should include pre-litigation legal advice to settle the dispute before the case is brought before the court, legal assistance in bringing the case before the court and representation in court, and assistance with or exemption from the costs of litigation" (recital 11 of the Directive).[58] The Directive notes the special dimension of pre-litigation legal advice, as a "preventive" instrument before the initiation of legal proceedings. In the implementation of these provisions, activities that fall within the framework of citizen advice can be included.

Indirectly, for the construction of a system of free pre-litigation legal aid, the following norms are important:

54 See also: P. Wiliński, P. Karlik, *Komentarz do art. 42 Konstytucji RP*, [in:] *Konstytucja RP*, t. 1, *Komentarz. Art. 1–86*, red. M. Safjan, L. Bosek, Warszawa 2016.

55 See also: T. Barankiewicz, *Etyczne treści prawa do dobrej administracji*, [in:] *System Prawa Administracyjnego*, t. 13, *Etyka urzędnicza i etyka służby publicznej*, red. R. Hauser, Z. Niewiadomski, A. Wróbel, Warszawa 2016, pp. 43–49.

56 Dz.Urz. WE L 26, s. 41.

57 Trociuk, *Pomoc*, p. 143.

58 Compare: Witkowska, *Przegląd*, pp. 5–6.

1. Council Directive 2005/85/EC of 1 December 2005 on the establishment of minimum standards on procedures in Member States for granting and withdrawing refugee status[59];
2. Directive 2013/32/EU of the European Parliament and of the Council of 26 June 2013 on common procedures for granting and withdrawing international protection[60];
3. Directive 2013/33/EU of the European Parliament and of the Council of 26 June 2013 on the establishment of standards for the reception of applicants for international protection[61];
4. Directive 2013/48/EU of the European Parliament and of the Council of 22 October 2013 on the right of access to a lawyer in criminal proceedings and in European Arrest Warrant proceedings and on the right to inform a third party of a deprivation of liberty and the right to communicate with third parties and consular authorities during a deprivation of liberty[62]; and
5. Directive of the European Parliament and of the Council (EU) 2016/1919 of 26 October 2016 on ex officio legal assistance to suspects and defendants in criminal proceedings and to requested persons in European Arrest Warrant proceedings.[63]

1.5. Summary

From the analysis, one should conclude that free pre-litigation legal aid does not derive directly from international documents. The norms of international and European law have the character of so-called minimum standards, which means that it is permissible to introduce at the level of national legislation norms that exceed the universal standards.[64] Thus, the norms indicated in the study (in particular: the Universal Declaration of Human Rights, the ICCPR, the ECHR or the CFR) are to some extent a point of reference for the creation of forms of free pre-litigation legal aid, especially in the context of ensuring that people in difficult life situations have access to free legal information on the effective realisation of the right to a court hearing (launching legal proceedings and asserting their rights). This applies first and foremost to those who are particularly

59 Dz.Urz. UE L 326, s. 13.
60 Dz.Urz. UE L 180, s. 60.
61 Dz.Urz. UE L 180, s. 96.
62 Dz.Urz. UE L 294, s. 1.
63 Dz.Urz. UE L 297, s. 1.
64 Całkiewicz and Rotkiewicz, *Prawo*, p. 541; Przybysz, *Prawo*, p. 350.

vulnerable to victimisation (e.g. suspects under the age of 18, persons who are unable to establish their own situation due to their health, foreigners, persons with disabilities, and indigent persons).[65] This is fundamental to ensuring the so-called "minimum standard" of the rights of the accused, in particular: the trial of cases within a reasonable time[66] and free access to a public defender when justified by the interests of justice (Article 6(3)(c) ECHR). From Articles 6 and 14 of the ECHR, there are positive obligations on states to guarantee effective and efficient protection of the individual and to build an effective system of legal aid to vulnerable persons in order to secure an effective right of access to court.[67] Such conclusions also follow from *soft law*[68] which, although not universally binding, perhaps should be read in terms of guaranteeing the widest possible group of persons in need of protection in the effective assertion of their rights.[69]

65 Zob. także: Trociuk, *Pomoc*, p. 142; Wąsek-Wiaderek, *Prawo*, pp. 359–360; Lipowicz, *O mądre*, pp. 314–315; Przywora, *Free*, p. 41.

66 W doktrynie szerzej: Waltoś, *Zasada*, p. 303; Mik, *Teoria*, p. 265.

67 Zob. także: Flaga-Gieruszyńska, *Idea*, p. 55.

68 Hałub, *Konstytucyjne*, p. 73.

69 Przywora, *Normatywny*, p. 136.

Chapter II. Free pre-litigation legal aid – an analysis of examples of selected legal systems

2.1. Swedish solutions

2.1.1. Preliminary remarks

As the first of these, we shall discuss the Swedish solutions. This is justified, on the one hand, by the legislative "maturity" of the solutions adopted in the Kingdom of Sweden and, on the other hand, by a system which, as a result of the evolution of pre-court legal aid solutions, has abandoned the concept of free advice in favour of a system of cost participation by the party. It should also be emphasised that this is an internationally well-established system. Hence, reaching to the solutions contained therein, in the opinion of the authors, is a valuable point of reference in terms of building an optimal model of free pre-litigation legal aid.

From the outset of the discussion, it should be emphasised that the Swedish legal system is quite peculiar, as it provides for a very broadly defined institution of legal aid in the form of legal advice, legal assistance and legal aid under the rules governing criminal and civil proceedings. In the late 1980s and early 1990s, it was regarded as one of the most generous systems in terms of available opportunities to receive unpaid legal aid. By contrast, however, there is no direct equivalent to the institution of civic counselling in Sweden.

2.1.2. Historical development of the institution of legal aid in Sweden

The first act on legal aid for poor people was adopted as early as 1919. However, the solutions it contained were somewhat residual.[1] Of more significance was the Legal Aid Act of 1 July 1973 (*Rättshjälpslagen*)[2] (hereinafter: RL 1973). The norms preceding the introduction of this law consisted of regulations enabling guarantees of exemption from court costs and the granting of a public defender in criminal cases in accordance with the Code of Judicial Procedure

1 I. Schoultz, *Legal Aid in Sweden*, [in:] *Outsourcing Legal Aid in the Nordic Welfare States*, red. O. H. Rønning, O. Hammerslev, Lund 2018, p. 45.

2 Rättshjälpslagen (1972:429).

(*Rättegångsbalken*).[3] Exemption from costs could be granted when a party could not cover the costs of the proceedings due to its financial situation.[4]

Legal aid could be provided in two forms. The first was the establishment of a legal aid institution at the local self-government level. At that time, the so-called *Jämtland* model was used. It was named after the county that first introduced it.[5] The idea was that legal aid was provided with financial support from the Swedish state in certain areas of counties and municipalities based on an agreement between the relevant local government unit and the Swedish Bar Association (*Sveriges Advokatsamfund*). The second form of assistance is legal assistance in court proceedings at the state-wide level.[6] However, it was emphasised that these were adopted at the local government level and thus did not have state-wide coverage. As already pointed out, this system was financed from local government funds.[7]

With the enactment of RL 1973, legal aid was introduced in four different forms:

1. general legal aid (allmän rättshjälp);
2. legal aid in criminal cases (rättshjälp åt misstänkt i brottmål);
3. legal aid by public counsel (rättshjälp genom offentligt bitrade); and
4. legal advice (rådgivning).

In addition, it was envisaged that the costs of defence counsel could be paid in administrative cases and in cases in which the plaintiff claimed benefits.[8] Such scattered assistance and the variety of its forms led to large budget expenditures. The draft explanatory memorandum to the draft of the new law on legal aid emphasised that in 1994–1995 alone the costs associated with this task totalled about SEK 870 million. These costs had yet to be augmented by other expenses such as chancery fees. The greatest attention was paid to criminal legal aid, which accounted for about SEK 364 million, and general legal aid, which accounted for about SEK 342 million.[9]

---

3 Rättegångsbalk (1942:740).

4 Regeringens proposition (Uzasadnienie do nowelizacji Instrumentu Rządzenia) 1996/97:9, p. 7.

5 P. S. Muther, *Reform of legal aid in Sweden*, "International Lawyer" 2020, nr 9(3), pp. 481–482, source: https://core.ac.uk/download/pdf/216914158.pdf (access: 05.12.2022).

6 Muther, *Reform*, pp. 482–484.

7 Muther, *Reform*, pp. 481–482.

8 Regeringens proposition 1996/97:9, pp. 78–79.

9 Regeringens proposition 1996/97:9, p. 79.

In this section, it is worth synthesising the aforementioned categories of legal aid. General legal aid was provided in cases involving individuals, as well as property protection cases. Exceptions were cases involving premarital agreements, real estate, when the plaintiff had legal aid insurance, as well as in cases where the plaintiff did not have a legitimate interest in the case. The limiting factor in such cases was income thresholds. Anyone with an annual income of more than SEK 249,000 was not entitled to legal aid. With a lower income, the state covered the costs of a professional attorney and other costs, such as taking evidence, among others. At the same time, the state did not cover reimbursement of litigation costs to the other party to the proceedings if the plaintiff lost the case.[10]

It is worth noting that in Sweden, legal aid implemented in the form of legal advice included the provision of legal advice or similar legal aid for a period not exceeding one hour. At the same time, legal advice could be given to any person regardless of income. Fees for the person providing legal advice were charged for each 15 minutes of advice started.[11]

Legal aid for suspects in criminal cases has been important. This is paid under the public defender formula under Chapter 21 of the Code of Judicial Conduct (*Rättegångsbalk*)[12] (hereinafter: RB). The issue of covering funds under criminal legal aid was based on both the Legal Aid Act of 1997 (*Rättshjälpslagen*) (hereinafter: RL 1997) under the so-called other legal aid, and other state sources.[13] The right to a public defender does not depend on the state of the suspect's personal finances.[14]

Another type of legal aid is that provided in cases involving a person's freedom of movement or physical integrity. Among these cases, cases involving psychiatric treatment, social welfare and the Law on Foreigners were most frequently indicated. This type of assistance – as with legal aid in criminal cases – was not determined by the property status of the beneficiary.[15]

At the same time, Swedish law included regulations for a public defender when legal aid was provided to victims of certain crimes under the Act of 26 May 1988 on Legal Aid for Victims of Crime (*Lagen om målsägandebiträde*).[16]

---

10 Regeringens proposition 1996/97:9, p. 79.
11 Proposition 1981/82: 28, p. 12.
12 Rättegångsbalk (1942:740).
13 Regeringens proposition 1996/97:9, p. 80.
14 Regeringens proposition 1996/97:9, p. 80.
15 Regeringens proposition 1996/97:9, p. 81.
16 Lagen om målsägandebiträde (1988:609).

This assistance was provided regardless of the income of the person to whom a public defender was appointed.[17] It is available to victims of more serious crimes such as assault, sexual offences and public disorder. At the same time, in the case of sexual offences, the plaintiff must in any case benefit from the legal assistance of the plaintiff, unless the circumstances of the case show that such assistance is not needed.[18] Funding for legal aid under the said law is based on the same principles as reimbursement for legal aid under the RL. With the reimbursement being based on the number of hours spent on the case.[19]

Until the adoption of the new law, the aforementioned forms of legal aid were amended several times and, for example, legal aid was allowed in premarital agreement cases. At the same time, restrictions were placed on receiving legal aid when a similar case was heard against the same person. Also eliminated was the possibility of providing legal aid in so-called pilot cases (*pilotfallen*) – in other words, preliminary rulings against proceedings that are already underway or will be initiated in the future. These were cases that depended on proceedings that were already underway or on a case that had already been decided, with the facts of the case remaining unchanged. This was a large number of cases involving the illegal circulation of drugs, and it was felt that in order to introduce budget savings, the possibility of providing legal aid in this type of case should be drastically reduced. The amendment introduced stipulated that legal aid could be postponed until the final resolution of a prejudgment in which the circumstances of the case and the claim asserted are identical. If, in such case, legal aid has been granted in the original case, which has a preliminary ruling, further legal aid in an identical case will be withheld, which does not preclude the state from covering the costs of legal aid at a later stage. Otherwise, legal aid will be fully paid for.[20]

Despite the changes, it was stressed that the new system requires a completely new approach. The most important argument cited was that it was too complicated and therefore difficult for citizens to access. It was also pointed out that difficulties in the structure of the organisation of legal aid generated problems in receiving legal aid and even finding a legal basis for providing it.

---

17 Regeringens proposition 1996/97:9, p. 80.

18 Brottsoffrets rättigheter, źródło: https://www.nck.uu.se/kunskapsbanken/amnesguider/rattsvasendets-ansvar/brottsoffrets-rattigheter/ (access: 06.12.2022).

19 Ersättning till målsägandebiträdet, SOU 2007:6, p. 315.

20 L. Heuman, *Rättshjälp och pilotfall*, SvJT 1983, p. 223.

Also, attention was drawn to the current system of financing legal aid, as being not very transparent and comprehensible to citizens.[21] Moreover, there were situations where different types of legal aid overlapped, which led to many practical difficulties,[22] especially at the settlement stage. Finally, the cost-intensity of this system was pointed out.[23] The legal aid system of that period was described as one of the most generous legal aid systems in the world.[24] It was emphasised that the Swedish solutions were assumed to be a safety valve for those seeking legal aid which, however, is not the case due to the difficulties of their operation in practice. Among the problems, it was also reported, in particular, the need to tighten the system, so that the person using it could get more than he was entitled to due to the proceedings, namely, earn.[25] All these arguments prompted a change in legal aid regulations, which was expected to contribute to the unification of the system and its transparency.[26]

As a result of the work on the new regulation, the Law on Legal Aid was adopted, which came into force on 5 December 1997. It was claimed as an objection that this reform, however, did not address the issue of legal aid in criminal proceedings and legal aid for victims of crime.[27]

2.1.3. Free legal aid under legal insurance

Free legal assistance was conceived as a special kind of safety valve in case the main instrument of assistance in the form of legal insurance – which most often took the form of a clause within the property insurance contract – did not work. It could also result from a separate legal insurance contract, which formed the basis for asking the insurer to provide legal assistance. According to this arrangement, legal insurance was an instrument of legal protection in Sweden. However, it should be noted, this was not a new solution, as it has been operating in the Swedish system since the 1960s.[28] In its original version, it was an instrument available alongside free legal aid. With the adoption of the new law, it was indicated that a person who has adequate insurance is no longer entitled to legal aid

21 Regeringens proposition 1996/97:9, p. 81.
22 Regeringens proposition 1996/97:9, p. 81.
23 Regeringens proposition 1996/97:9, p. 82.
24 Schoultz, *Legal*, p. 46.
25 Regeringens proposition 1996/97:9, p. 82.
26 Regeringens proposition 1996/97:9, p. 83.
27 Schoultz, *Legal*, p. 46.
28 Regeringens proposition 1996/97:9.

under RL 1997 for matters covered by insurance. The rationale for this was that the insurance was in effect in civil cases pending before the courts of general jurisdiction, in the land courts and before the Supreme Court, which provided legal assistance to citizens in a wide range of cases.[29]

Legal insurance has different forms and serves different purposes (e.g. it is available for disputes related to real estate and other property). It is regulated in the Insurance Business Act of 22 December 2010. (*Försäkringsrörelselag*)[30] and the Law on Certain Contractual Provisions for Legal Protection Insurance of 2 December 1993 (*Lag om vissa avtalsvillkor för rättsskyddsförsäkring*).[31]

2.1.4. The institution of legal advice

The RL 1997 contains arrangements for legal aid and legal advice (§ 1 of the RL 1997). Legal advice is the first step towards receiving legal aid. At the same time, it is not a rule. Legal advice can be understood as consultation or the first step towards receiving legal aid.[32] The Swedish solutions in RL 1997 do not include a definition of legal advice, but only an indication that it is provided on the basis of a fixed fee.[33] It is assumed that the purpose of this institution is to obtain information about a person's further legal options and the acceptability of receiving assistance under the legal aid institution.[34]

In order to receive legal aid, legal advice is required to provide at least one hour of legal advice on a given case, unless such advice is clearly unnecessary or there is another special reason for not providing it (§ 1 RL 1997). In this case, legal advice was described as a kind of safety valve against the provision of legal aid, which generated greater costs for the state.[35] However, a person could be exempted from this obligation in special cases. Examples of situations in which prior legal advice was not required were, for example, a case in which the person had received legal information elsewhere and had extensive knowledge of the general legal situation, or when the case was a continuation of an earlier proceeding (e.g. when a claim for damages was separated from a criminal case and the public

29 Schoultz, *Legal*, pp. 48–49.
30 Försäkringsrörelselag (2010:2043).
31 Lag om vissa avtalsvillkor för rättsskyddsförsäkring (1993:1303).
32 Utvärdering av rättshjälpslagen (Ocena ustawy o pomocy prawnej) (1996:1619), Rapport, del A, p. 8.
33 Utvärdering av rättshjälpslagen (1996:1619), Rapport, del A, p. 50.
34 Utvärdering av rättshjälpslagen (1996:1619), Rapport, del A, p. 52.
35 Utvärdering av rättshjälpslagen (1996:1619), Rapport, del A, p. 43.

defender became a legal aid person RL 1997). Such an arrangement was also permitted in situations where court deadlines were running out or negotiations were to be conducted that required an immediate response.[36]

Such a solution can be seen as a kind of "compromise" in response to proposals to introduce legal advice as a mandatory element within the system of providing legal aid to individuals. During the development of this solution, the Gothenburg Court of Appeals questioned the assumption that legal advice was to be a mandatory element of the provision of legal aid. Such assistance is not always required and is not even always relevant, especially in cases involving administrative proceedings.[37] However, the exemption from the need for prior legal advice is among the exceptions to the requirement for prior advice, which was also the legislator's assumption.[38]

The obligatory nature of legal advice was viewed positively, as it allowed for the receipt of general information about the case and thus improved the provision of legal aid. However, the lack of functionality of providing free legal assistance in a case that resulted in a settlement[39] was also highlighted. However, it was commented that, in practice, people do not apply for exemption from legal advice, because it is too time-consuming and requires submission of the relevant forms, which further complicates the entire procedure.[40]

Attention should be paid to the practice of the institution responsible for dispensing with the need for prior legal advice, the Legal Aid Council (*Rättshjälpsnämnden*). For example, this Council has granted the request of a mother who brought an action to establish paternity and where persons who are Swedish citizens have applied for benefits in Sweden. As an example of another case, the situation of a person struggling with an impairment whose health deteriorated significantly during the period of the dispute was highlighted, indicating that legal advice was not needed.[41] A rather interesting case involved a person who lived abroad and requested legal assistance directly, bypassing legal advice. The Council refused to skip the legal advice stage on the grounds that the fact of being in another country does not constitute a serious reason within the meaning of

36 Utvärdering av rättshjälpslagen (1996:1619), Rapport, del A, p. 41.
37 Regeringens proposition 1996/97:9, p. 104.
38 Utvärdering av rättshjälpslagen (1996:1619), Rapport, del A, p. 9.
39 Regeringens proposition 1996/97:9, p. 106.
40 Utvärdering av rättshjälpslagen (1996:1619), Rapport, del A, p. 46.
41 Utvärdering av rättshjälpslagen (1996:1619), Rapport, del A, p. 43.

RL 1997, since legal advice assistance can be obtained both by telephone and by letter.[42]

The institution of legal advice was regulated in Section 4(1) of RL 1997, according to which advice is provided on legal matters by a lawyer or legal assistant in a law office for a maximum of two hours. It was stressed that this time was sufficient and that the cost of the advice must favour its availability.[43]

It has been accepted that advice may also be given by a person designated as an assistant in the provision of legal aid. An assistant within the framework of legal assistance may be designated as a lawyer, an assistant lawyer in a law firm, or another person who is qualified to perform duties within the framework of legal advice (Section 24 (1) RL 1997). If justified by the circumstances of the advice, it is permissible to dismiss the assistant. Section 2 of this paragraph indicates that a legal assistant may be changed upon special authorisation and only for special reasons.

Advice within the framework of legal advice may be provided for an appropriate fee, but it must be at a level that allows easy access to the advice (§ 4 (2) RL 1997). At the same time, it is permissible to reduce the fee or waive it altogether if the financial situation of the person seeking advice requires it. In the event that the person seeking assistance is a minor then the advice is completely free of charge (§ 4(3) RL 1997).

The rates for legal advice fees are set by the government or a body designated by the government issuing more detailed regulations on counselling fees and reductions in counselling fees in this regard (Section 4(4) RL 1997). Fees for legal advice are charged for each 15 minutes of counselling started.[44]

It is worth noting the explanatory memorandum to the draft RL 1997, which emphasises that advice under the institution of legal advice is provided for virtually all categories of cases. At the same time, this assistance is available to both individuals and legal entities regardless of income. However, the catalogue of matters that make it possible to receive advice within the framework of legal advice excludes matters related to the preparation of tax returns, relating to the administration of record and registration matters in accordance with the Land Code.[45]

---

42 Case number RN 363/1998.

43 Utvärdering av rättshjälpslagen (1996:1619), Rapport, del A, p. 8.

44 Regeringens proposition 1996/97:9, p. 104.

45 Regeringens proposition 1996/97:9, p. 104.

Where legal advice is a mandatory stage of legal aid, it is transferred, as it were, to the free legal aid case and is therefore not separately included in statistics, for example.

2.1.5. The institution of legal aid

The main issue is a discussion of the rules that condition the granting of legal aid, that is, the specific grounds for granting it (§ 10–13 RL 1997). Legal aid may not be granted in cases involving, among others:

1. preparation of a tax return, premarital agreement, will or donation;
2. administration of claims from the inheritance estate;
3. debt restructuring;
4. concerning real estate;
5. asset declarations;
6. asset valuation; and
7. property division cases.

Sweden has adopted a catalogue of cases in which legal aid may be granted: these are cases involving divorce and related matters, child support, taxes, duties, fees or security for payment of taxes, duties and fees. Legal aid may also be granted to a person who is not a citizen of Sweden, but when the case will be heard in a Swedish court (§ 11 RL 1997). In proceedings heard abroad, legal aid may be granted to a person who is a resident of Sweden (§ 12 RL 1997).

Sweden has also adopted categories of cases in which legal aid is not granted. It may not be granted to a person who is or was an entrepreneur, in a case arising in the course of a business activity, unless there are special reasons for doing so as to the nature and limited scope of the activity, or the financial situation of the entrepreneur (§ 13 RL 1997). In the event of the death of a person to whom legal aid has been granted, the aid shall pass to the heir along with the estate, if the testator so requests, taking into account the nature and importance of the case, as well as the financial situation of the owners of the estate, the state may participate in the costs under legal aid (§ 14 RL 1997).

In addition, additional legal aid is provided to victims of sex crimes when the case is to be tried abroad (§ 21 RL 1997). In this type of situation, the state undertakes to bear the costs of the assistance and the evidence and investigation that would be necessary to exercise the rights of the plaintiff, as well as the travel and living expenses of the plaintiff and his or her guardians or other persons who must be present for an appearance in court or before another authority.

This provision applies only if the person does not have legal insurance (Section 22 RL 1997).

Conditions for receiving legal aid are derived from the RL 1997 Act. Legal aid may be granted to an individual whose annual income does not exceed SEK 260,000 (§6). Legal aid may be granted if the plaintiff needs legal assistance in addition to advice that cannot be satisfied in any other way (§ 7). This assistance may be granted only if, due to the nature and importance of the case, the value of the subject matter of the litigation and the general circumstances justify the state's share of the costs (§8).

It is worth noting that Swedish legislation has not completely adopted free legal aid. A person receiving such assistance is required to contribute an appropriate amount depending on the value of the subject matter of the dispute (§ 23 RL 1997). The percentage distribution of the contribution is regulated as follows:

1. 2% of costs if the value of the legal aid does not exceed SEK 50,000;
2. 5% of the costs, but not less than SEK 500, if the value of the subject of the dispute exceeds SEK 50,000 but does not exceed SEK 100,000;
3. 10% of the costs, but not less than SEK 1,000, if the value of the subject of the dispute exceeds SEK 100,000, but is not more than SEK 120,000;
4. 20% of the costs, but not less than SEK 1,500, if the value of the subject of the dispute exceeds SEK 120,000, but is not more than SEK 150,000;
5. 30% of the costs, but not less than SEK 2,000, if the value of the subject of the dispute exceeds SEK 150,000, but is not more than SEK 200,000; and
6. 40% of the costs, but not less than SEK 5,000 if the value of the subject of the dispute exceeds SEK 200,000.

Legal aid may be granted only if, due to the nature and importance of the case, the value of the subject matter of the dispute and the general situation, the state's share of the costs is justified (§ 8 RL 1997). In order to receive legal aid, the applicant should fill out the appropriate form posted on the website of the courts of general jurisdiction at.[46]

Thus, the Swedish approach provides for the participation of the person in the costs of legal aid. Therefore, it is not justified in this case to use a term closer to the Polish system, namely "free legal aid". At the same time, it should be noted that the Swedish legislator did not exclude the possibility of complete exemption from the costs of legal aid, as is the case with legal advice.

46 See https://www.domstol.se/tjanster-och-blanketter/rattshjalp/ (access: 17.11.2020 r.).

2.1.6. Bodies within the legal aid and legal advice system

The Legal Aid Council is responsible for legal aid issues. It consists of a chairman who is or was a regular judge,[47] two members who have legal training, and two other members. All members must be Swedish citizens. They are appointed by the government for a fixed term (§ 48 RL 1997).

The Council's activities were regulated by the Regulation on Instructions for the Legal Aid Council of 22 November 2007. (*Förordning med instruktion för Rättshjälpsnämnden*)[48] (hereinafter: Instruction I). It is responsible for handling appeals under RL 1997 (§ 1 Instruction I). According to § 44 of RL 1997, the Council handles, among other things, appeals against decisions issued by the Legal Aid Authority (*Rättshjälpsmyndigheten*). Administrative support for the Council is the responsibility of the Court of Appeals for Nedre Norrland in accordance with § 5 of Instruction I.

The activities of the aforementioned Legal Aid Authority[49] are regulated by the Regulation of 22 November 2007 concerning the Instructions for the Legal Aid Authority (*Förordning med instruktion för Rättshjälpsmyndigheten*)[50] (hereinafter: Instruction II). It is responsible for handling certain matters in accordance with RL 1997, such as: for example, reimbursement for providing legal advice and processing reimbursement issues under RL 1997. The Legal Aid Authority ultimately determines the legal aid fee payable to the plaintiff after determining the remuneration of the person who provided the legal aid (Section 1 of Instruction II).[51]

It is headed by the President of the District Court in the City of *Sundsvall* (§ 2 of Instruction II). He may delegate an employee of the court's administration to perform tasks in the administration of the body (§ 4 Instruction II).

The Legal Aid Authority also conducts relatively extensive information activities on legal aid matters for courts and attorneys, as well as litigants and the public. Outreach activities also include providing information regarding the conditions for obtaining legal aid.[52]

---

47 To see more information about profession of judge in Sweden see: B. Przywora, A. Wróbel, *Status prawny sędziego w Królestwie Szwecji*, [in:] *Status prawny sędziego. Państwa europejskie*, t. 1, red. B. Przywora, Warszawa 2019, pp. 405–427.

48 Förordning med instruktion för Rättshjälpsnämnden (2007:1079).

49 Przywora, *Normatywny*, p. 318.

50 Förordning med instruktion för Rättshjälpsmyndigheten (2007:1078).

51 Sveriges Domstolar årsredovisning 2019, p. 75.

52 Sveriges Domstolar årsredovisning 2019, p. 75.

2.1.7. Statistical approach

In the first year of RL 1973, 25,000 pieces of legal advice were provided, half of which involved compensation for reduced or waived fees. On the other hand, in the years of the start of RL 1997, that is, 1993–1994, the number of cases in which legal advice was given was 1,987. At the same time, it was stressed that this was not an accurate figure, as it did not include cases that turned into legal aid. One wonders what the reason for the lower quantity of advice given compared to the first years of RL 1973 might be. It was assumed that this could have been the result of a lack of proper communication to the public about the possibility of using such a facility. Another potential reason could have been the need to introduce a fee.[53]

The inability to accurately check current statistics on the use of legal advice is cited as a flaw in the Swedish system, as there are no separate statistics on the provision of legal advice to individuals without further request for legal assistance. It was reported that in the year 2000, 6,400 people used legal aid and all of these people also used the institution of legal advice, which was described as a rather high rate.[54]

2.1.8. Conclusions

Legal advice has been legally merged with the institution of legal aid. The issue of fees has also been considered within the framework of legal advice. The Swedish Bar Association, in a report, proposed that the fee for legal advice be counted as a fee under legal aid. However, this approach has been criticised on the grounds that the purpose of these fees is to counteract the rampant use of advice when it is not needed. According to the government, this was not appropriate.[55] It was questioned whether the fees for legal advice were too high. Speaking on this issue, the government indicated that the amount did not seem high. In addition, it was pointed out that most people go to court very rarely. It was stressed that, on average, a statistical citizen has to deal with the court once or, exceptionally, twice in his life. Moreover, the fees still seem low and accessible. In addition, it was mentioned that the fee can be reduced at the same time, or people can be exempted from paying the fee.[56]

---

53 Utvärdering av rättshjälpslagen (1996:1619), Rapport, del A, p. 42.

54 Utvärdering av rättshjälpslagen (1996:1619), Rapport, del A, p. 53.

55 Regeringens proposition 1996/97:9, p. 107.

56 Utvärdering av rättshjälpslagen (1996:1619), Rapport, del A, p. 58.

2.2. Ukrainian solutions

2.2.1. Preliminary remarks

In Ukraine, there is no direct equivalent to the institution of civic counselling. The closest institution is the so-called primary free legal aid (orig. безоплатна первинна правова допомога).

The modern system of free legal aid is the result of transformations that took place in the 1990s. At that time the state pursued a similar direction of development of this assistance to that of solutions adopted in Western European countries. The final goal is to harmonise as closely as possible with the solutions adopted in European countries' systems.[57]

The Ukrainian legislator pays careful attention to the institution of free legal aid. It serves to deliver state policy, as it is broadly defined, in the area of social policy. This institution finds its basis in the Constitution of Ukraine and is developed in legislation. At the constitutional level, a separate Article 59 of the Constitution of Ukraine (*Конституція України*)[58] (hereinafter: the Constitution) is devoted to it, and the detailed rules of its organisation are derived from statutes. The main one is the Law of 9 July 2011 on Free Legal Aid (*Закон України Про безоплатну правову допомогу*)[59] (hereinafter: the Law on Legal Aid). This law has been amended several times, particularly during the period of armed aggression by the Russian Federation.

2.2.2. Constitutional empowerment of the institution of free legal aid

Article 59 of the Constitution guarantees everyone the right to legal aid; although, on the other hand, attention should be drawn to the reference that in cases regulated at the level of the law, such aid may be provided free of charge (Article 59, first sentence of the Constitution). In addition, the article emphasises the important role of the Bar in the realisation of this right, particularly in ensuring the right to defence and to receive legal assistance in proceedings before courts and other state bodies (Article 59, second sentence of the Constitution).

---

57 Ю.О. Данилевська, Л.В. Павлик, З.З. Петрович, У.О. Цмоць, *Право особи на б езоплатну правову допомогу*, Львів 2018, p. 26.

58 Конституція України, Відомості Верховної Ради України (ВВР), 1996, № 30, ст. 141.

59 Закон України “Про безоплатну правову допомогу”, Відомості Верховної Ради України (ВВР), 2011, № 51, ст. 577).

The protection of human and civil rights is one of the most important elements of the functioning of a democratic state. The guarantee of realisation of this right is also expressed at the level of legal aid, which can be implemented in various forms, such as providing consultations, explanations, assistance in drafting lawsuits and applications, statements and complaints, providing representation before the courts and before other state bodies, as well as through legal assistance in criminal proceedings.[60] With this approach, free legal aid is similar to the solutions adopted in Poland.

The right to legal aid ranks as a fundamental human right in Ukrainian law. According to Article 59(1) of the Constitution, the right to legal aid is granted to every person. The use of the word "any" (*кожен*) means that the right is enjoyed by Ukrainian citizens, stateless persons and foreigners residing on Ukrainian territory. It is emphasised that the right to legal aid is based on the principle of equality of all persons before the law and the prohibition of discrimination on the basis of race, colour, religion and political views.[61]

Important for the constitutional determination of the status of the right to legal aid was the decision of the Constitutional Tribunal of Ukraine of 30 September 2009. № 23-рп/2009.[62] In its analysis, the Constitutional Tribunal interpreted Article 59 of the Constitution and pointed out that the right to legal aid plays an important role in the protection of human rights and freedoms. The Constitutional Tribunal stressed that ensuring the right to legal aid requires the state to ensure that every person has access to such aid. Such obligations should be implemented through the adoption of relevant laws and sub-legislative acts aimed at creating conditions for the realisation of the right to legal aid. The court argued that the realisation of this right is twofold. On the one hand, it can serve as a preventive mechanism against situations of potential threat of restriction of citizens' rights and freedoms, and on the other hand, it is an instrument for protecting a person in case of violation of his rights and freedoms.

According to Article 64 of the Constitution, the right to legal aid cannot be restricted and is directly applicable under Article 8(3) of the Constitution. This

---

60 В.Я. Тацій (ред.), Конституція України. Науково-практичний коментар, Харків 2011, p. 686.

61 Тацій (ред.), *Конституція*, p. 688.

62 Рішення Конституційного Суду України у справі за конституційним зверненнямг ромадянина Голованя Ігоря Володимировича щодо офіційного тлумачення положень статті 59 Конституціїї України (справа про право на правову допомогу) від 30.9.2009 р., № 23-рп/2009, Вісник Конституційного судуУкраїни-2009 р., № 6, с. 32.

formulation of the right to legal aid creates a kind of "safety valve" in the event that the state fails to enact relevant laws or sub-statutory acts (failing to ensure the realisation of the right to defence).[63] From Article 59 of the Constitution derive, on the one hand, guarantees for the provision of legal aid, and on the other, obligations for their implementation imposed on state institutions. The state is obliged to construct a model for providing this assistance, that is, appropriate institutional organisation. A distinction should be made between state bodies and other entities that, as part of their duties, are obliged to provide legal aid. The first category includes the Ministry of Justice of Ukraine, the Ministry of Labour and Social Policy, among others. The second category includes the notary and the bar (for proceedings before courts and state bodies). Further entities are business legal entities that are engaged in providing legal assistance as part of their activities. Legal aid is also provided by local government units.[64]

2.2.3. Legal basis for the implementation of free pre-litigation legal aid

The legal basis for the implementation of the provision of free legal aid is the Constitution and the Law on Aid, which was enacted in 2011. It has been amended several times to adapt the form of legal aid to the challenges of the time.[65]

Of primary importance is the scope of this assistance. Free legal aid can be provided to natural persons (Article 2 of the Law on Aid). The use of the term "natural person" indicates, as already mentioned, that this includes Ukrainian citizens, foreigners and persons without citizenship, which is consistent with Article 59 of the Constitution. The range of persons authorised to grant it also follows from this regulation: both natural persons and legal entities conducting charitable activities in accordance with their internal regulations. At the same time, Article 2(1) of the Law on Aid provides for the division of free legal assistance into primary free legal assistance and secondary free legal assistance (безоплатна вторинна правова допомога). In view of the subject of this study, the implementation of primary legal aid is of fundamental importance.

This assistance is regulated in Chapter II of the Law on Aid. Primary legal aid, is a type of guarantee by the state, which consists of informing a person about his rights and freedoms, how to exercise them, possible actions when these rights

63 Тацій (ред.), *Конституція*, pp. 689–690.

64 Тацій (ред.), *Конституція* p. 692.

65 The list of changes is on the website: https://zakon.rada.gov.ua/laws/show/3460-17#Text (access: 03.12.2022 r.). The last amendment took place on May 3, 2022.

have been violated, and the procedure for appealing against decisions of state and local government bodies, complaints against the actions or inaction of state and local government bodies, as well as against the actions of public officials (Article 7 (1) on legal aid).

From Ukrainian regulations, there are broad limits to the concept of primary legal aid. This translates into the application of the law. For example, attention should be paid to how the forms of this assistance may be implemented:

1. legal information;
2. legal consultation and clarification of specific legal issues;
3. preparation and filing of relevant motions, complaints and other legal documents (at the same time, the law excludes from the scope of original legal aid any documents in proceedings before the court);
4. providing consultations, clarifications and preparing draft agreements for the use of land plots, which include leasing, renting, etc., for villagers who own the said properties; and
5. providing assistance in ensuring access to secondary legal aid and mediation.

Particular attention should be paid to Article 7 (1) para. 3–1 of the Law on Aid, concerning consultations in the area of agricultural real estate. There is a new category of cases as a result of the reform of Ukraine's land resources and the possibility of privatising state land. This topic is very controversial, and the process is considered extremely complicated; thus, introducing the possibility of receiving free legal assistance in this sphere is a response to indicated needs.[66]

Legal aid is provided to all persons subject to the jurisdiction of Ukraine. Article 3 of the Law on Legal Aid explicitly cites the Constitution of Ukraine as the determinant of the scope of subjects entitled to free legal aid. Free legal aid may be provided at the request of an adult (Article 8 of the Law on Legal Aid). Minors may request such assistance from their legal representatives (Article 10, paragraph 2 of the Legal Aid Law). In the case of persons who are totally or partially incapacitated, they may receive free legal assistance upon application by their legal guardians or curators (Article 8 (3) of the Legal Aid Law).

Executive authorities and local government bodies should specify the hours and days of reception when a person can personally appear at a certain place and receive advice under free legal aid (Article 11 of the Law on Aid).[67] This

66 See https://www.legalaid.gov.ua/novyny/na-odeshhyni-tryvaye-informatsijna-kampaniya-z-pytan-zemelnoyi-reformy/ (access: 20.11.2020).

67 A map of free legal aid points and their hours of operation are available at: https://www.legalaid.gov.ua/statistics/ (access: 21.11.2020).

assistance is provided on an on-call basis. An interested party may receive free legal assistance from a highly qualified employee, who should provide appropriate assistance in a precise and accessible manner. It is important to determine the manner in which assistance is provided, as this determines the effectiveness of the solutions adopted by the legislator. Interestingly, in addition to personal contact, such assistance can also be received electronically, after filling out the appropriate form on the website of the Coordination Centre for Free Legal Aid,[68] as well as by telephone or through appropriate instant messengers.

The means for providing legal assistance remotely became particularly important during the war period. The main method of remote communication is by telephone. Within the framework of legal aid provided in this form, a person can receive assistance through consultation and clarification of specific legal issues. This is a toll-free line that operates from 8 a.m. to 7 p.m. on weekdays and from 9 a.m. to 5 p.m. on Saturday and Sunday.[69] In addition, a telephone number has been set up for people abroad to call.

Subsequently, a legal aid question can be asked via a bot on the *Telegram* messenger app. At the same time, there is also a separate channel on *Telegram* aimed at people who have been victims of violence.[70] In addition, for the most topical issues, any person can reach out to the instructions on the *WikiLegalAid* website[71] or the phone app "Free Legal Assistance" (*Безоплатна правова допомога*) or "Your Law" (*Твоє право*).[72]

In order to receive assistance under free legal aid, an interested person should apply to the relevant governmental or local authorities. These bodies are obliged to provide appropriate legal assistance within 30 days of receiving the application for free legal assistance. At the same time, this deadline is limited to 15 days, in accordance with Article 10 (5) of the Law on Aid, if the provision of free legal assistance is to consist in the provision of legal information.

The law has introduced a kind of "fuse" against abuses in the provision of free legal aid – a ban on charging any fees for its provision. The Ukrainian legislator has introduced a ban on charging fees for the very act of providing legal aid, as

68 See also: https://www.legalaid.gov.ua/zvernennya/onlajn-yurydychna-konsultatsiya/ (access: 05.12.2022).

69 Допомога онлайн, source: https://legalaid.gov.ua/kliyentam/yak-otrymaty-bezoplatnu-pravovu-dopom/ (access: 07.12.2022).

70 Ibidem.

71 https://wiki.legalaid.gov.ua/.

72 Допомога онлайн, source: https://legalaid.gov.ua/kliyentam/yak-otrymaty-bezoplatnu-pravovu-dopom/ (access: 07.12.2022).

well as for issuing application forms, certificates and other letters. This solution is clearly intended to ensure the actual free nature of legal aid when it is provided in practice (Article 10(6) of the Law on Aid).

In the event that the institution responsible for providing legal aid finds that the application falls outside the scope of free legal aid, it is obliged to refer the case to the competent authority within five calendar days and notify the applicant (Article 10, paragraph 7 of the Law on Aid). This solution is necessarily intended to promote the final provision of legal assistance to the person by the competent authority, as well as to bring about the settlement of the case.

When assistance should be provided under so-called secondary legal aid, the institution to which the person has applied is obliged to provide information about the possibility of secondary legal aid and how to obtain it (Article 10 (8) of the Law on Aid). If an employee providing advice on primary free legal assistance within reception hours comes to the conclusion that assistance should be provided under secondary legal assistance, he may provide such legal assistance, and he is obliged to notify the person requesting assistance (Article 11 (4) of the Law on Aid).

The Ukrainian legislature stipulated in Article 30 of the Law on Aid that in the event of refusal to provide primary free legal assistance by executive authorities, local government bodies, as well as institutions providing primary free legal assistance, then the party who has been refused assistance is entitled to turn to the court with a complaint. A complaint to the court can also be made against the inaction of those providing free legal aid, both secondary and primary.

The Law on Aid lays down the rules for financing this task with budgetary funds within the framework of financing the activities of executive authorities and territorial budgets (Article 29 of the Law on Aid).

2.2.4. Bodies responsible for providing free legal aid

Implementation of the provisions of Article 59 of the Constitution is carried out through the relevant state bodies. The constitutional regulation of legal aid is developed in Article 9 of the Law on Aid, which stipulates that at the primary level, free legal aid is provided by executive authorities, local government bodies, individuals, legal entities and by specialised institutions. In the case of secondary legal aid, it is also provided by centres for providing free secondary legal aid and by attorneys listed in the register of attorneys who provide such assistance.[73]

---

73 Register available at: https://www.legalaid.gov.ua/advokatam/reyestr-advokativ/ (access: 23.11.2020).

The central body responsible for the implementation of free legal aid is the Coordination Centre for the Provision of Free Legal Aid, established within the Ministry of Justice to effectively manage the system of free legal aid. This body was established by the Decree of the Council of Ministers of 6 June 2012 on the functioning of the Coordination Centre for the provision of free legal aid.[74] This institution is responsible for providing organisational, informational and material-technical support to implement the tasks of the Ministry of Justice in the sphere of free legal aid. Its duties also include keeping registers of attorneys and institutions that can provide secondary free legal aid, and monitoring the practice of the application of the provisions on this assistance, as well as signalling proposals for changes in state policy in this area (paragraph 12 of this regulation).

The directory of entities providing secondary free legal aid is maintained by state bodies. This issue does not raise any major doubts. On the other hand, the catalogue of entities providing primary free legal aid is more extensive and in practice some difficulties arise as to the formation of its final form. This includes discussions regarding the category of legal entities conducting charitable activities. Ukrainian legislation in this regard is extremely elaborate and often excludes from this activity many organisations that in fact provide such assistance.[75]

Specialised bodies are considered to be, among other things, institutions established by local government bodies that provide primary legal assistance. Article 12 of the Aid Law has its development in the Local Government Law of 21 May 1997 (*Закон України Про місцеве самоврядування*)[76] (hereinafter: Local Government Law). Article 26 item 39-1 of the Local Government Law provides that local government bodies shall establish institutions providing free legal aid and finance them from the local government budget.

Local government bodies also have responsibilities related to selecting and dismissing the heads of these institutions, as well as determining the rules for participation in the provision of free legal assistance by individuals and legal entities. According to Article 38 of the Local Government Law, within local

---

74 Постанова Кабінету Міністрів України від 6 червня 2012 р. № 504 Положення про Координаційний центр з надання правової допомоги.

75 К. Струкова, Особливості організації надання безоплатної правової допомоги недержавними суб'єктами, Актуальні проблеми правознавства. Випуск 2 (10). 2017 р., рр. 35–37.

76 Закон України "Про місцеве самоврядування" (Відомості Верховної Ради України (ВВР), 1997, № 24, ст.170).

government, those authorised to carry out the broadly defined activities related to the establishment of institutions providing free legal aid include the executive bodies of village and municipal councils. These tasks relate not only to the creation of said bodies, but also to inform citizens about the possibility of free legal aid.[77] In practice, free legal aid is provided by citizens who have completed higher legal studies. It is permissible to specify additional requirements that must be met by a candidate for the person who will provide such assistance.[78]

Local government bodies may conclude an agreement with legal entities that, according to their statutes, may provide free legal assistance. Such agreements are concluded either for an indefinite period of time or for a fixed period of time and assume the provision of free legal aid within the jurisdiction of the local government. The procedure for concluding an agreement with external entities is determined by the Ministry of Justice.[79] As part of the implementation of primary legal aid tasks, local governments may entrust the performance of duties to attorneys or legal persons with whom a contract has been concluded for the provision of free legal aid (Article 12 (8) of the Law on Aid).[80]

Lawyers and the Ukrainian Bar play an important role in providing secondary legal assistance. According to Article 2 of the Law on Bar and Bar Activities of 5 July 2012. (*Закон України про адвокатуру*)[81] (hereinafter: the Law on Bar), the Bar of Ukraine is a non-state self-governing institution that provides defence, presents interests and provides legal assistance, as well as independently determining issues related to its organisation and structure. According to Article 6 of the Law on Bar, an advocate may be a natural person who has a university degree in law from a Ukrainian university or a foreign university that is recognised by Ukraine, speaks the Ukrainian language, has at least two years' experience, has

77 А. Сербіна, *Надання безоплатної правової допомоги органами місцевого* самоврядуванння, Місцеве самоврядування-2017,-№ 12, https://i.factor.ua/ukr/journals/ms/2017/december/issue-12/article-32589.html (access: 20.11.2020).

78 Сербіна, *Надання.*

79 Наказ 15.06.2012 № 891/5 Про затвердження Порядку та критеріїв залучення органами місцевого самоврядуваня юридичних осіб приватного права до надання безоплатної первинної правової допомоги.

80 Сербіна, *Надання.*

81 Закон України про адвокатуру та адвокатську діяльність (Відомості Верховної Ради (ВВР), 2013, № 27, ст.282).

passed the relevant exam and has received a certificate on the right to practice as an advocate.[82]

2.2.5. Statistics on the effectiveness of primary free legal aid

It is important to highlight the practical functioning of the free legal aid system by taking statistics into account. Under the latest statistics for the period from 1 November 2015 to 30 November 2022, legal aid was requested 3,918,419 times. The aforementioned number includes 3,477,412 referrals who ended up with an explanation or consultation by an employee of the legal aid centre, as well as 441,466 cases where it was decided to refer cases to secondary legal aid. For the indicated period, 2,591,106 people received legal aid.[83]

In 2019, a total of 623,977 requests for legal aid were made, of which 558,160 resulted in consultations and 65,817 in referrals for secondary legal aid. In 2020 (as of 23 November 2020) a total of 465,289 legal aid applications were accepted, of which 417,520 cases ended in consultations and 47,769 ended in referrals for secondary free legal aid.[84]

In the following year, 2020, there were 568,931 requests for assistance. Of this number, 510,118 cases were given explanations and consultations under primary legal aid. In the remaining cases, secondary legal assistance was provided, that is, in 58,813 cases.[85]

Going forward, in 2021, legal aid centres were approached 713,202 times, with consultation and clarification provided in 627,281 cases, while in the remaining 85,921 cases, secondary legal aid was granted.[86]

---

82 More (including on historical development) see: О. Гець, *Історичний та сучасний погляди на надання безоплатної правової допомоги адвокатами*, Юриспреденція: теорія і практика 2011, № 11, pp. 23–27.

83 Статистична інформація роботи системи безоплатної правової допомоги, source: https://legalaid.gov.ua/STATYSTYCHNA-INFORMACZIYA-ROBOTY-SYSTEMY-BEZOPLATNOYI-PRAVOVOYI-DOPOMOGY/ (access: 28.11.2022).

84 See https://www.legalaid.gov.ua/statistics/ (access: 30.11.2022).

85 Статистична інформація роботи системи безоплатної правової допомоги, source: https://legalaid.gov.ua/statystychna-informacziya-roboty-systemy-bezoplatnoyi-pravovoyi-dopomogy/ (access: 04.12.2022).

86 Ibidem.

In 2022, as of 30 November 2022, the number of registered requests for legal assistance was 504,779, of which 459,158 cases were provided with explanations and consultations. In the case of 45,158 people, secondary legal aid was provided.[87]

There are also mobile free legal aid points in Ukraine. Statistics show that one in 12 of every piece of advice is provided just within the framework of mobile free legal aid points in small towns. In the first six months of 2019, 43,300 people benefited from such a form.[88] In the current situation, mobile points have gained great importance as they are opened in the so-called points of unbreakability[89] (пунктах незламності).[90]

The most common range of cases requested by citizens includes issues of agricultural law, family law and administrative law.[91] It seems interesting to juxtapose the ranges of cases for which citizens turned to the legal aid centres in 2021, a year in which the centres were approached a record number of times, and in one of the most difficult years for independent Ukraine – 2022.

Civil law and civil procedure cases dominated in 2021 – 141,747 cases. Another category was family law cases – 98,459 cases, and administrative law and administrative proceedings cases – 83,730, followed by housing law – 65,339 cases, inheritance law – 60,530 cases, agricultural law – 51,625 cases and social welfare cases – 49,226.[92]

The situation changed slightly in 2022. The largest number of cases in which legal aid was provided was in civil law and civil proceedings – 83,473, followed by administrative law and administrative proceedings – 81,543, family law – 69,067, another category, social welfare cases – 60,850 and labour law – 34,977 cases.[93]

It can be seen from the above that there has been a significant increase in the number of cases in the field of administrative law and administrative procedure,

---

87 Ibidem.

88 See https://www.legalaid.gov.ua/novyny/kozhna-12-ta-pravova-konsultatsiya-nadayetsya-cherez-dystantsijni-ta-mobilni-punkty-dostupu/ (access: 19.11.2020).

89 These are places where every person can warm up, charge a phone, etc. They were created in response to the destruction of Ukraine's energy infrastructure by the Russians.

90 Source: https://legalaid.gov.ua/novyny/bezoplatna-pravova-dopomoga-u-punktah-nezlamnosti/ (access: 13.12.2022).

91 See: https://www.legalaid.gov.ua/statistics/ (access: 23.11.2020).

92 Статистична інформація роботи системи безоплатної правової допомоги, source: https://legalaid.gov.ua/statystychna-informacziya-roboty-systemy-bezoplatnoyi-pravovoyi-dopomogy/ (access: 04.12.2022).

93 Ibidem.

as well as in the category of social welfare cases. These changes are most likely due to the war on Ukrainian territory.

The activities of the free legal aid centres also include informational meetings on current legal and social issues. Examples of the topics of information meetings within the framework of free legal aid are: informing people about the reliefs they are entitled to, for example, for families with many children[94]; informing citizens about their rights vis-à-vis debt collection companies[95]; pointing out possible paths for resolving land disputes[96]; meetings organised for soldiers to inform them about their rights.[97]

2.2.6. Conclusions

The solutions adopted in the Ukrainian system are characterised by a very wide range of possibilities for receiving legal aid. Despite the fact that the system is relatively new, due to its being in operation on Ukrainian territory for fewer than 10 years, it has a solid structural foundation. The active operations of the Coordination Centre for the Provision of Free Legal Aid is evident, among other things, by holding a large number of meetings with citizens and organising mobile advice points.

Legal aid regulations in Ukraine provide a number of failsafes for the implementation of legal aid tasks, in the form of administrative liability for failure to properly implement these tasks. This is an understandable solution to counter possible abuses.

In times of war, legal aid is needed as never before, and it is indeed fulfilling its role. Legal aid centres and the institution of legal aid itself has proven to be an extremely flexible instrument that can be easily adapted to the reality surrounding citizens. It can be a place where legal aid is provided to soldiers and

---

94 See: https://www.legalaid.gov.ua/novyny/yaki-pilgy-nadayutsya-bagatoditnym-bat kam/ (access: 08.12.2022).

95 See: https://www.legalaid.gov.ua/novyny/yaki-diyi-kolektoriv-slid-vvazhaty-nepravo mirnymy-ta-yaki-prava-vony-mayut-vidnosno-borzhnykiv-obgovoryly-v-oleksandr iyi/ (access: 08.12.2022).

96 See: https://www.legalaid.gov.ua/novyny/zeme lni-superechky-kudy-zvertatysya/ (access: 09.12.2022).

97 https://legalaid.gov.ua/novyny/ozbroyuyemo-vijskovosluzhbovcziv-pravovymy-znannyamy/ (access: 05.12.2022).

their families, and it can also be a place that will support people in their search for missing loved ones.

2.3. Solutions in the United Kingdom of Great Britain and Northern Ireland

2.3.1. Preliminary remarks

The system of legal aid and civic counselling in the United Kingdom of Great Britain and Northern Ireland (hereinafter: the UK) is considered one of the exemplary and leading in the world. It is mentioned that there is a division of legal aid at the level of litigation, at the level of providing appropriate legal advice to determine the further course of action and the further procedure, and in the form of civic counselling[98] (citizens' advice). There is a system of legal aid or legal representation referred to as *legal aid* throughout the Kingdom. The designed solutions are intended to provide assistance to low-income people to ensure the realisation of the individual's rights to a fair trial.[99]

The basic principle of the legal aid system in the Kingdom is to outsource tasks to organisations and provide funds to carry out this task in the form of grants. As a result, it is practically entirely based on the outsourcing system. Legal aid at the judicial level is provided for civil and criminal cases. The central act regulating such arrangements is the *Legal Aid, Sentencing and Punishment of Offenders Act 2012.*[100]

In order to receive assistance in criminal or civil court proceedings, the case should concern an individual person and should be qualified as suitable for such assistance due to its legal nature. Also of significance is the person's income, which must not exceed a certain threshold. This is referred to as the *means and merits test*. The assessment of the reasonableness of the award comes down to two stages of scrutiny. The first is the determination of monthly income. It is assumed that free assistance is granted to those with a monthly income that does not exceed GBP 2,657 gross.[101] However, this does not mean that a person will

---

98 See: https://www.nidirect.gov.uk/articles/legal-aid-schemes (dostęp: 03.12.2022).

99 See: https://e-justice.europa.eu/content_fundamental_rights-176-ew-pl.do?member=1 (access: 03.12.2022).

100 Legal Aid, Sentencing and Punishment of Offenders Act 2012, UK Public General Acts 2012 c. 10.

101 Ministry of Justice, Annex C The Current Legal Aid Financial Eligibility Rules – Summary, https://consult.justice.gov.uk/digital-communications/legal-aid-eligibil

receive legal assistance when this condition is met, as the second stage of control is triggered. This involves checking whether the person has capital or owns real estate or movable property whose value exceeds GBP 3,000 in criminal cases and GBP 8,000 in civil cases. In the case of legal aid in certain types of civil cases and after a certain income threshold is exceeded, the person participates in the financing of legal aid (*contribution*).

The basic principles for making an assessment for the award of legal aid are regulated, among others, in the Lord Chancellor's April 2014 Guidance to Determining Financial Eligibility for Certified Work (*Civil Representation Guide to Determining Financial Eligibility for Certified Work – April 2014 v1*)[102] and in criminal cases under the Lord Chancellor's May 2020 Guidance Under Section 4 of the Legal Aid, Sentencing and Punishment of Offenders Act 2012. (*Lord Chancellor's Guidance Under Section 4 of the Legal Aid, Sentencing and Punishment of Offenders Act 2012*).[103]

Legal assistance can be provided in various forms: direct contact (*face to face*), as well as through a hotline or through an online application.[104]

Legal aid in criminal cases is granted to persons against whom criminal proceedings have been initiated. For criminal cases before magistrates' courts, the person's income threshold test combined with the interest of justice in providing assistance (*financial means and interests of justice test*) is applied. On the other hand, for cases before the Crown Court, only the financial threshold test applies accordingly.[105]

From the point of view of this study, an important component of the system of assistance provided to people in the Kingdom is *Citizens Advice*. Mention should be made of *Citizens Advice Scotland*, *Citizens Advice Northern Ireland* and their offices at the local level. Refugee assistance institutions also play an

---

ity-and-universal-credit/supporting_documents/annexcsummaryofcurrentlegalaidfinancialeligibilityrules.pdf (access: 01.12.2022).

102 See https://assets.publishing.service.gov.uk/government/uploads/system/uploads/attachment_data/file/332853/legal-aid-guide-to-determining-eligibility-certificated-work.pdf (access: 29.11.2022).

103 See https://assets.publishing.service.gov.uk/government/uploads/system/uploads/attachment_data/file/885341/lord-chancellors-guidance-under-section_4-laspo_May_2020.pdf (access: 30.11.2020).

104 See https://www.gov.uk/guidance/legal-aid-submit-a-claim#how-to-claim-online (access: 29.11. 2022 r.).

105 See https://e-justice.europa.eu/content_fundamental_rights-176-ew-pl.do?member=1 (access: 01.12.2022 r.).

important role, among them the *Refugee Legal Central* and the *Immigration Advisory Service.*[106]

2.3.2. Evolution of citizens' advice

The institution of citizens' advice in the Kingdom is best illustrated in the words of David Harker[107]:

> As a nationwide network, Citizens' Advice serves to provide advice to everyone and on every possible issue under the sun, and since its early years it has had a unique insight into emerging trends and identified the pressing problems that everyday life brings. Counselling not only allows specific cases to be dealt with based on the experiences of real people, but also makes visible the trends that are occurring in particular regions and throughout the country.[108]

The need for the establishment of citizens' advice was raised in the Kingdom back in 1924 in the so-called *Betterton Report on Public Assistance*. With the spectre of war looming and the experience of World War I, a conference of social organisations was held in 1938 to clarify issues related to possible difficulties in family life and the threat posed by a potential war. It was decided that the state should be prepared for the coming challenges.[109] Accordingly, a network of Citizens' Advice Offices was established in major cities and industrial towns where the threat of war was expected to be most acute.[110]

On 3 September 1939, 200 offices were established, which were managed by the *Central Committee in London.*[111] By the end of the war there were more than 1,000 of them. Various social organisations were involved in the process of establishing the offices, as well as local bodies, which for many years played an important role in the financing of citizens' advice. Each office was independent in its operations and was linked by the State Welfare Board. This body received funds

---

106 See https://e-justice.europa.eu/content_fundamental_rights-176-ew-pl.do?member=1 (access: 01.12.2022 r.).

107 Chief Executive of Citizens Advice from 1997 to 2010.

108 M. Zucker, *The British "Citizens' Advice Bureaus"*, "Social Service Review" 1950, nr 24(1), p. 89.

109 Zucker, *The British*, p. 89.

110 G. Fisher, *Advice on Everything. A History of the Citizens Advice Service in Harrow, 1939–2009*, source: https://citizensadvice.citizensadvice.org.uk/harrow_cab_history.pdf (access: 24.11.2020).

111 See https://www.cas.org.uk/about-us/citizens-advice-scotland/our-history (dostęp: 06.12.2022).

from the government and was responsible for their redistribution.[112] The offices were set up in public and private buildings.[113] After the bombings, due to the lack of premises, the offices often operated directly on the streets.[114]

In their early days, the offices dealt with assistance on war-related issues, such as instructing how a citizen should proceed after a city was bombed, and providing assistance in searching for missing loved ones. A large part of the offices' activities also concerned income tax and employment issues.[115] Over time, as the offices gained the trust of citizens, they became a place where many people went to ask for advice on matters beyond just everyday life. These included questions about family matters.[116] This presents a picture of an institution available to any person in any category of issues.

The offices are an excellent example of institutions that were established during the war period and have survived to this day, as the work they do has been shown to have many benefits for society.[117] Certainly, this approach to citizens' advice was motivated by its popularity. For example, in 1948 the office received as many as 1,500,000 questions. This number increased in 1949. At that time, cases mainly concerned housing issues, family matters and personal problems, as well as social security, that is, issues important in daily life.[118]

The further development of citizens' advice and its financing from the very beginning depended, among other things, on the level of interest from the public, which in turn was based on the difficulties faced by citizens. This was reflected in the degree of state funding for citizens' advice. It was pointed out that in the 1950s, despite the positive reception of the institution of citizens' advice, funding was reduced, resulting in a reduction in the number of offices. On the other hand, due to the adoption of new housing laws, the number of questions

112 Zucker, *The British*, p. 89.

113 Famously, there was a mobile office in a box for transporting horses; *History of the Citizens Advice service*, source: https://www.citizensadvice.org.uk/about-us/how-citizens-advice-works/who-we-are-and-what-we-do/history-of-the-citizens-advice-service/#:~:text=4%20September%201939%3A%20The%20first,relatives%20and%20prisoners%20of%20war (access: 25.11.2020).

114 D. Korman Sloviter, *Let's Look at Citizens Advice Bureaux*, "American Bar Association Journal" 1979, nr 65(4), p. 568.

115 See https://www.cas.org.uk/about-us/citizens-advice-scotland/our-history (access: 06.12.2022).

116 Korman Sloviter, *Let's*, p. 568.

117 Zucker, *The British*, p. 89.

118 Zucker, *The British*, p. 89.

in citizens' advice bureaux increased significantly, and in response to greater demand in 1960, state funding increased again. Since the 1970s, consumer protection has been a very important theme in citizen assistance. This contributed to an increase in the number of questions in citizens' advice bureaux.[119] For example, the increase in the need for citizens' advice in specific localities was the result of protests by postal workers and the crisis at *Rolls Royce*. In addition, there was an amendment to family law, specifically divorce laws.[120]

However, state support for citizens' advice has not always matched the increase in interest from citizens. In the 1980s, due to the economic crisis, the demand for counselling increased, but funding dropped significantly.[121] The examples given confirm that citizens' advice was one of the instruments that provided a real response to the needs of society.

2.3.3. Citizens' advice – basic assumptions

The functioning of citizens' advice is based on four principles: free-of-charge status, independence, confidentiality of advice and impartiality.

It is particularly important to be independent within the framework of the offices' activities, due to the fact that they often act against state bodies. Most frequently, such assistance may consist, among other things, in helping to draft an appeal against a decision by a pension authority, in helping to collect evidence by contacting offices or health institutions.[122]

In addition to the principles mentioned, an holistic approach to counselling is also important. It assumes that counsellors at the first conversation assess all problems and inquire whether the client has any additional difficulties about which advice can be given.[123]

Certainly, the most important aspect of civic advice activities is to directly assist citizens by giving them advice. An integral role of the counselling offices from the very beginning has also been to analyse the effectiveness of the legal solutions adopted. An expression of this activity was lobbying for changes in the law at governmental or parliamentary level. The greatest achievement of citizens'

---

119 History of the Citizens Advice service....

120 Fisher, *Advice.*

121 Fisher, *Advice.*

122 S. Kirwan, M. McDermont, J. Clarke, *Imagining and practicing citizenship in austere times: The work of Citizens Advice*, "Citizenship Studies" 2016, nr 6–7(20), p. 766.

123 M. McDermont, *Citizens Advice in austere times*, [in:] *Reflections on challenging times for advice agencies*, ed. S. Kirwan, Advising in austerity, Bristol, 2017, p. 32.

advice in this field is considered to be bringing about the adoption of the aforementioned legal aid regulation in the Kingdom.[124]

2.3.4. Procedure for the provision of citizens' advice

Of primary importance is the subjective scope of citizens' advice, that is, who can receive such assistance. It is emphasised that with citizens' advice, the definition of the term "citizen" is not specified. On the other hand, official documents do not use the term "citizens" to describe people who receive citizens' advice. For example, the term "clients" is used. It is indicated in practice that no attempt has been made to define this term either. This is probably due to the assumption that a citizen in the sense of citizenship counselling is "any person who crosses the threshold of the office".[125] Consequently, counselling assistance is available to any person, regardless of whether or not he or she is a citizen of the Kingdom.

The procedure for receiving citizens' advice usually consists of several steps. If it is the first time a person comes to a citizens' advice office, he or she should make an application at the reception desk and fill out the appropriate form regarding contact information and whether the case has already been the subject of counselling. In addition, the form includes consent for the processing of personal data and a separate consent for future contact to continue the case. The Citizens' Advice website includes a guide to the necessary documentation that a person should bring with them when coming to the facility. The manual includes a breakdown of specific types of cases. For example, in labour law cases, these should include a copy of the employment contract, letters received from the employer, and proof of income (such as tax returns).[126]

The first meeting is held with the counsellor and is of an introductory (familiarisation) nature. It lasts about 15 minutes. The counsellor asks a few questions to clarify how assistance can be provided and, consequently, either gives advice or indicates an appropriate solution. No prior appointment is required for this type of meeting, it is enough to appear at the relevant office.[127]

---

124 M. Zucker, *Citizens' Advice Bureaus: The British Way*, "Social Work" 1965, nr 10(4), p. 88.

125 Kirwan, McDermont and Clarke, *Imagining*, pp. 770–771.

126 See e.g. https://www.citizensadvice.org.uk/about-us/how-we-provide-advice/what-to-bring-on-your-local-citizens-advice-visit/ (access: 6.12. 2022).

127 See *What to expect from your visit*, https://www.citizensadvicesurreyheath.org.uk/get-advice/face-to-face/what-to-expect-from-your-visit/#:~:text=Your%20first%20meeting%20with%20an,issue%20forward%20or%20resolve%20it (access: 6.12. 2022).

If this meeting proves insufficient, the general counsel schedules an appointment for *advice appointments*. These appointments last about an hour, and their purpose is to examine the case more closely due to the circumstances involved. As a result of this meeting, the counsellor should prepare an action plan to clarify the case. Part of the plan may also include another meeting or a referral to another specialised organisation.[128]

A counsellor can be any person. As a rule, he or she does not need to have a legal background, since legal advice is not provided as part of citizens' advice. However, as an additional service, citizen counselling may take the form of a 15-minute meeting with a lawyer who will provide legal advice. With the prerequisite being a prior visit to a general counsel, who can refer the person to speak with a lawyer.[129]

Citizens' advice is also allowed to provide home visit counselling to people who are unable to appear in person or use online contact due to health, age or obligations. In cases where a person requests assistance because he or she is unable to support him or herself and has no money for food, the counsellor can make a referral to a local food bank. In special cases, a counsellor can refer a person to organisations that help socially isolated people or people with emotional difficulties.[130] Counsellors can also collect feedback on experiences with health care workers and then forward them to the relevant authorities. Another additional service is to help people experiencing domestic violence, who can call a designated number and apply to the court for an appropriate emergency ruling.[131]

Solutions to the counselling process are subject to criticism. In practice, it is pointed out that due to the large number of cases and funding difficulties, the activity of citizens' advice is largely automated. As mentioned, the first meeting lasts about 15 minutes, which leads to a situation in which it is unlikely to provide comprehensive advice. Consequently, this can also distort the basic principle of an holistic approach to solving citizens' problems.

---

128 See What to expect from your visit....

129 See What to expect from your visit....

130 More: https://www.citizensadvicesurreyheath.org.uk/social-prescribing/ (access: 6.12. 2022).

131 More additional services available on the website: https://www.citizensadvicesurreyheath.org.uk/additional-services/ (access: 07.12.2022).

2.3.5. Organisation of citizens' advice

The central institution responsible for legal aid in England and Wales is the Lord Chancellor, while its organisation is handled by the *Legal Aid Agency* (hereinafter: LAA). This entity can commission legal aid in a certain category of cases under grants as one of its tasks under special advice.

Citizens Advice consists of a network of local organisations that are supported by Citizens Advice and Citizens Advice Scotland, as well as Citizens Advice Northern Ireland.[132]

When asked about the structure of the citizens' advice office, one of the directors of the local citizens' advice office stated: "The office stands and falls on its own feet," with which he wanted to emphasise their independence and loose connection to both Citizens Advice and the government or local authorities.[133]

At the beginning of their existence, offices were established spontaneously by the local community and their employees were instructed by consultants. Often, they were formed on the basis of meetings of a few people, which then turned into meetings of many. If there was interest, a local advisory committee was formed to find a suitable room, search for resources, organise training and seek volunteers.[134] In turn, each local committee was represented on a regional committee, which sent representatives to the state-wide committee. The regional committees consisted of lawyers, social workers, civil servants, businessmen, and employees of health and education authorities. The central body was the State Board of Social Guidance Offices, which had a secretariat. Their duties included: organising conferences, promoting the establishment of new offices, constructing training programmes and collecting information from local organisations. Funding for the Board came partly from the Government and the rest from private sources.[135]

At present, Citizens Advice is registered as a charity and as a company limited to a guaranteed sum. In turn, all local citizens' advisory boards are members of Citizens Advice. The acts that regulate the activities of counselling at the state and local levels are the memorandum and statute.[136]

---

132 McDermont, *Citizens*, p. 31.

133 Zucker, *Citizens' Advice*, p. 87.

134 Zucker, *Citizens' Advice*, p. 87.

135 Zucker, *Citizens' Advice*, p. 88.

136 See Annual report 2019/20, p. 54, source: https://www.citizensadvice.org.uk/Global/CitizensAdvice/Governance/Annual%20Report-2019-20.pdf (access: 07.12.2022). See https://www.cas.org.uk/about-us (access: 07.12.2022 r.).

Counselling is provided by entities that are organised as charities under the Charities Act of December 2011. (*Charities Act*).[137] Their structure has also been organised in this way. Interestingly, when analysing the composition of the people who sit on the board of trustees of these companies, it is very important whether the person is part of the local community in which the office operates. These are usually people born in a particular locality, or people who have lived in a particular place for many years.[138]

As for the status of the offices themselves, they invariably remain autonomous, of course. Regarding the relationship between local offices and state-level guidance organisations, their cooperation is based on providing support and resources, as well as upholding the standards of civic assistance.[139]

As for the general counsellors, they are mostly volunteers. Their training takes place at the local level using resources and materials provided by Citizens Advice, Citizens Advice Scotland and Citizens Advice Northern Ireland. It takes about nine months to train a volunteer. After six months, the volunteer is already providing advice as part of general counselling, but under the supervision of more experienced and specialised counsellors who are employed within the local Citizens Advice office.[140]

Training of people for specialised counselling is done by external entities and at the state level. Nationwide organisations also post guidance for counsellors on their websites. It is indicated that they are intended to perpetuate certain practices.[141]

In addition, in support of local offices, organisations at the state level influence local offices by conducting regular audits of cases handled by the office. Assistance in this form is considered particularly necessary, as it improves the work of the offices and enhances the quality of advice provided. The result of the audit may be a decision on the next audit, such as next year or as late as three years from now.[142]

Citizens' advice is facing a large number of impediments, especially of a financial nature, as well as due to financial cuts in civil legal aid, which means that

137 Charities Act 2011, UK Public General Acts 2011 p. 25.

138 See https://www.citizensadvicesurreyheath.org.uk/about-us/whos-who/ (access: 07.12.2022 r.).

139 McDermont, *Citizens*, p. 38.

140 McDermont, *Citizens*, p. 38.

141 McDermont, *Citizens*, pp. 31–35.

142 McDermont, *Citizens*, p. 35.

interest in counselling is growing, but at the same time its capacity is not developing due to funding shortages. In order to make citizens' counselling work, many offices are either merging, downsizing or closing.[143] There are currently 270 citizens' advice locations in England and Wales[144] and 59 in Scotland.[145]

2.3.6. Financing of citizens' advice activities

Funding for citizens' advice services takes place at several levels. From the very beginning of their existence, the relevant local authorities were involved in their financing (through grants). However, the situation has changed and local authorities are contributing less and less to the funding of counselling. This makes the offices, as part of their activities, forced to organise collections and apply for small grants, as well as receive funds from donations from city councils and parish councils.[146] It is becoming a fairly daily situation to receive funding from private sponsors such as global corporations.[147]

Some offices receive funding to provide legal aid after signing a contract with the Legal Services Committee. Under this contract, the offices also provide legal aid. However, it must be stressed that this is not a reliable source of funding due to budget cuts for the entire legal aid system.[148]

Wanting to give an idea of the funding structure, in 2019–2020, for example, the service's income amounted to £139.1 million, of which, among other things, £34.3 million was received from the Ministry of Work and Pensions, £24.4 million from the Money and Pensions Service, £16 million from the Ministry of Business, Energy and Industrial Strategy, and £11 million from the Ministry of Justice. However, it should be pointed out that these amounts were higher than in the previous year.[149]

2.3.7. Challenges for citizens' advice

One of the biggest challenges facing citizens' advice is the lack of adequate funding and the need to constantly seek new sources of funding. In each case,

143 McDermont, *Citizens*, pp. 31–32.

144 Annual report 2019/20…, p. 7.

145 See https://www.cas.org.uk/about-us (access: 08.12.2022).

146 McDermont, *Citizens*, p. 36.

147 See https://www.thirdsector.co.uk/citizens-advice-3m-funding-facebook/finance/article/1523782 (access: 08.12.2022 r.).

148 McDermont, *Citizen*, p. 36.

149 Annual report 2019/20…, p. 44.

it tends to be ad hoc funding provided through temporary projects. This may lead to a lack of in-person counselling, and over time – due to the need to cut costs – it will be replaced entirely by hotlines and contact via remote communication means. It is stressed that this could be a reason for the erosion of the basic premise of citizens' advice – an holistic approach to the problems faced by a person seeking advice. Another issue of concern is that the function of citizens' advice offices as a liaison in indicating needed changes in the law is under threat. This task has been jeopardised due to clauses in grant agreements with the government that prohibit the use of funds received from the government to either lobby for new legislation or to influence parliament, local authorities and political parties. In practice, this deprecates the possibility of performing one of the basic tasks of citizen advice – capturing and promoting favourable changes in the law.[150]

2.3.8. Statistical approach

A report on the activities of the Citizens' Advice Offices indicated that in 2019 there were 950 employees at the central level and 6,300 at the local level. As for volunteer statistics, they consist of 18,300 volunteers at the local level and 3,000 in individual programmes, such as criminal witness assistance.[151] On the other hand, the 2021–2022 report indicates that the number of people employed has increased to 1,000 employees at the central level and 7,700 at the local level. By contrast, the number of volunteers decreased to 16,700.[152]

In 2019 and part of 2020, advice was provided to more than 2.8 million people, among whom 1.3 million received help with face-to-face contact, 1 million people received help via hotlines and 483,000 people received consumer assistance. There is also significant growth in counselling provided via email and online chats, which have benefited 423,000 people. On the other hand, the criminal witness assistance programme benefited 97,000 people.[153] The most frequent requests from citizens were for help with consumer, debt, housing and employment law issues.[154] In turn, a total of 2.550 million pieces of advice were

150 McDermont, *Citizens*, p. 40.

151 Annual report 2019/20…, p. 7.

152 Citizens Advice annual report 2021/2022, p. 9, source: https://assets.ctfassets.net/mfz4nbgura3g/5piAqpbrv71hBujORjhM9r/b578b9b5057e545e91ec833e38076ece/Annual_Report_2021_22.pdf (access: 13.12.2022).

153 Annual report 2019/20…, p. 12.

154 Annual report 2019/20…, p. 12.

provided in the 2021–2022 period. Of this number, 1.96 million pieces of advice were provided by phone, 624,000 in response to questions directed by email, 183,000 pieces of advice were provided through personal contact and 176,000 through online chat available on the Citizens' Advice website.[155]

The 2019–2020 report on the activities of the counselling offices emphasises that the work of the offices contributes to large savings for both citizens and the state itself. According to the adopted conversion rate, for every £1 spent on Citizens' Advice, clients receive £12.60; in turn, from the point of view of the state budget, there are savings of £685 million per year. If these figures were combined, the value added to society from Citizens' Advice activities would be GBP 4 billion per year.[156] For the period 2021–2022, the figures looked even more promising. For every £1 spent on Citizens' Advice, advice office clients received an average of £14. In turn, the state budget saved as much as £717 million through the work of the offices. After combining these amounts, the value added from Citizens' Advice activities amounted to GBP 4.6 billion for the period under review.[157]

2.3.9. Conclusions

The solutions adopted in the Kingdom can serve as an example (model) for the operation of citizen counselling. Over the long years of its existence, it has become part of the Kingdom's society and inspires confidence among citizens. This is confirmed by the increasing statistics in the number of counselling services provided. As a result, the demand for such services is increasing.

Citizens' Advice also has an important function in the process of lobbying for the adaptation of existing laws to needs and challenges, and is a "natural intermediary" between citizens and state institutions, government and parliament.

However, an important problem in the implementation of citizens' advice remains the provision of stable funding. This factor will determine the functioning of this solution in the future. As a positive indicator, increased funding should be considered, which has allowed for the hiring of more staff in 2021–2022.

155 Citizens Advice annual report 2021/2022, p. 11, source: https://assets.ctfassets.net/mfz4nbgura3g/5piAqpbrv71hBujORjhM9r/b578b9b5057e545e91ec833e38076ece/Annual_Report_2021_22.pdf (access: 13.12.2022).

156 Annual report 2019/20…, p. 14.

157 Citizens Advice annual report 2021/2022, p. 12 źródło: https://assets.ctfassets.net/mfz4nbgura3g/5piAqpbrv71hBujORjhM9r/b578b9b5057e545e91ec833e38076ece/Annual_Report_2021_22.pdf (access: 13.12.2022).

Chapter III. Polish solutions

Preliminary remarks

The issue of free legal aid in Poland in its broadest sense as an instrument in the implementation of guarantees of a fair trial has been the subject of many studies.[1] Within the framework of this study, we focus our attention on the formalised model of free pre-litigation legal aid[2] (including covering solutions for

---

1 See in the literature in particular: G. Rząsa, *Konstytucyjne aspekty pomocy prawnej udzielanej osobom ubogim*, „Przegląd Legislacyjny" 2005, nr 3–4; S. Trociuk, *Pomoc prawna dla osób ubogich jako forma zapewnienia skutecznego dostępu do krajowego i europejskiego wymiaru sprawiedliwości*, [in:] *Dostęp obywateli do europejskiego wymiaru sprawiedliwości*, red. H. Izdebski, H. Machińska, Warszawa 2005; J. Barcik, T. Srogosz, *Prawo dostępu do adwokata w Polsce w świetle dyrektywy 2013/48/UE*, „Palestra" 2015, nr 7–8; A. Bisztyga, *Prawo do rozpatrzenia sprawy w rozsądnym terminie. Nowe działania: ADR, e-sąd*, [in:] *Transformacja systemów wymiary sprawiedliwości*, t. 2, *Proces transformacji i dylematy wymiaru sprawiedliwości*, red. J. Jaskiernia, Toruń 2011; D. Całkiewicz, A. Rotkiewicz, *Prawo pomocy jako gwarancja prawa do sądu dla najuboższych w świetle prawa międzynarodowego i unijnego oraz w przepisach ustawy – Prawo postępowaniu sądowoadministracyjnym*, [in:] *Dziesięć lat polskich doświadczeń w Unii Europejskiej. Problemy prawnoadministracyjne*, t. 2, red. J. Sługocki, Warszawa 2014; K. Flaga-Gieruszyńska, *Idea pomocy prawnej z urzędu w postępowaniu cywilnym*, [in:] *Aequitas sequitur legem. Księga Jubileuszowa z okazji 75. urodzin Profesora Andrzeja Zielińskiego*, red. K. Flaga-Gieruszyńska, G. Jędrejek, Warszawa 2014; J. Winczorek, *Dostęp do prawa. Ujęcie socjologiczne*, Warszawa 2019; J. Winczorek, *Public interest and access to justice: A liminal analysis*, „Archiwum Filozofii Prawa i Filozofii Społecznej" 2020, nr 3, pp. 24–40; W. Florczak, *Nieodpłatna pomoc prawna w Polsce. Systemowa analiza interdyscyplinarna*, Kraków 2021.

2 See in the literature in particular: K. Bandarzewski, *Udzielanie nieodpłatnej pomocy prawnej jako zadanie zlecone powiatowi*, [in:] *Charakter i konstrukcja zadań samorządu terytorialnego*, red. M. Stec, S. Płażek Warszawa 2017; O. Hałub-Kowalczyk, *Sformalizowany model dostępu do nieodpłatnej pomocy prawnej na etapie przedsądowym w Polsce*, Wrocław 2019; O. Hałub, *Konstytucyjne gwarancje prawa do nieodpłatnej pomocy prawnej na etapie przedsądowym*, „Forum Prawnicze" 2016, nr 4; M. Jabłoński, *Prawo do nieodpłatnej pomocy prawnej jako „element treści konstytucyjnego prawa do sądu" – uwagi na te postanowień ustawy z 5 sierpnia 2015 r. o nieodpłatnej pomocy prawnej oraz edukacji prawnej*, [in:] *Ochrona praw człowieka. Zagadnienia praktyczne*, red. A. Hauser, M. Urbaniak, Poznań 2019; A. Klich, *Idea pomocy prawnej w sprawach cywilnych a działalność klinik prawa*, [in:] *Aequitas sequitur legem. Księga Jubileuszowa z okazji 75. urodzin Profesora Andrzeja Zielińskiego*, red. K. Flaga-Gieruszyńska, G.

civic counselling, or legal advice, and their ways of financing and methods of quality verification). Of primary importance is the Law of 5 August 2015 on free legal aid, free civic counselling and legal education[3] (the Law on Free Legal Aid or LFLA).[4] Prior to its enactment – due to growing public demand – various forms of counselling were being developed (e.g. implemented by the Ombudsman, the Ombudsman for Children, social insurance companies, poviat consumer ombudsmen, parliamentary and senatorial offices, professional associations of lawyers, legal advisors, notaries, university legal clinics).[5] Hence, the emergence of a legal regulation providing for a formalised model of free pre-litigation legal aid, although long awaited by various circles, was not accepted uncritically.[6]

Jędrejek, Warszawa 2014; I. Lipowicz, *O mądre prawo i wrażliwe państwo*, Warszawa 2013; A. Ploszka, *Publicznoprawny status jednostki skrajnie ubogiej*, Warszawa 2019; B. Paxford, R. Rynkun-Werner, M. Wasylkowska-Michór, *Ustawa o nieodpłatnej pomocy prawnej oraz edukacji prawnej. Komentarz*, Warszawa 2016; S. Płażek, *Nowe usługi powiatu w zakresie nieodpłatnej pomocy prawnej*, [in:] *Działalność gospodarcza jednostek samorządu terytorialnego. Dopuszczalność i granice jej prowadzenia*, red. M. Stec, M. Mączyński, Warszawa 2016; B. Przywora, *Free legal assistance as an instrument in protecting the right of foreigners in the Republic of Poland – a contributions to the discussion*, „Roczniki Administracji i Prawa" 2020, nr XX(1); B. Przywora, *Normatywny model przedsądowej nieodpłatnej pomocy prawnej w Polsce*, Warszawa 2019; B. Przywora, A. Wróbel, *Poradnictwo obywatelskie w świetle badań prawnoporównawczych*, Warszawa 2020, https://iws.gov.pl/wp-content/uploads/2021/01/IWS_Przywora-B.-Wróbel-A._Poradnictwo-obywatelskie-w-świetle-badań-prawnoporównawczych.pdf (access: 24.06.2022 r.); T. Schimanek, *Możliwości wsparcia bezpłatnego poradnictwa obywatelskiego i prawnego przez samorządy lokalne*, p. 81, http://www.obywateliprawo.isp.org.pl/files/cke/Moliwoci....pdf (access: 25.06.2022 r.); J. Winczorek, *O potrzebie badań empirycznych nad dostępem do prawa*, „Państwo i Prawo" 2016, nr 12.

3 Tekst jedn. Dz. U. z 2021 r. poz. 945.

4 See in the literature in particular: Hałub O., *Konstytucyjne gwarancje prawa do nieodpłatnej pomocy prawnej na etapie przedsądowym*, „Forum Prawnicze" 2016, nr 4; B. Przywora, *Normatywny model przedsądowej nieodpłatnej pomocy prawnej w Polsce*, Warszawa 2019.

5 F. Czernicki, *Dostęp do nieodpłatnej przedsądowej pomocy prawnej w Polsce*, [in:] *Prawo wobec problemów społecznych. Księga jubileuszowa Profesor Eleonory Zielińskiej*, red. B. Namysłowska-Gabrysiak, K. Syroka-Marczewska, A. Walczak-Żochowska, Warszawa 2016, pp. 914–915.

6 E.g. F. Czernicki, *Dostęp*, p. 922.

As the practice of the formalised model of free pre-litigation legal aid in Poland shows, it is a challenge,[7] especially during the COVID-19 pandemic.[8]

In Poland, the introduction of a legal aid system stems both from ratified international documents and from the Constitution of the Republic of Poland.[9] In this part of the work we will discuss the constitutional basis and the statutory provisions arising from the law on free legal aid. In the final part, we will present the practical aspects of the implementation of the task of free legal aid, also taking into account the period of the COVID-19 pandemic. This period is legitimately considered an unprecedented event in the global world. It is necessary to emphasise the particularity of this epidemiological threat, determining the lives of all individuals and societies without exception.[10]

3.1. Free pre-litigation legal aid - comments from the perspective of the Polish Constitution

Access to the law is taken broadly as the actual ability of citizens with the help of legal tools to solve life problems.[11] Thus, it also includes the pre-trial stage. However, the Constitution of the Republic of Poland does not explicitly guarantee a universal subjective right to pre-trial free legal aid. An analysis of its norms allows the conclusion that many instruments (including free pre-litigation legal aid) can provide real assistance in the effective assertion of individual freedoms and rights. All the more so, since Article 80 of the Constitution of the Republic of Poland implies the right of everyone to apply, on the terms set forth in the law, to the Ombudsman for assistance in protecting their freedoms or rights violated by public authorities.[12] Consequently, free pre-litigation legal aid is an instrument in the realisation of the right to court and social justice (which finds

7 See szerzej: P. Chmielnicki, *System (bez)prawnej pomocy, czyli jak rząd Ewy Kopacz poradził sobie z nadprodukcją prawników*, [in:] *Fenomen prawa administracyjnego. Księga jubileuszowa Profesora Jana Zimmermana*, red. W. Jakimowicz, M. Krawczyk, I. Niżnik-Dobosz, Warszawa 2019, pp. 113–127; M. Stefaniuk, *Społeczna potrzeba nieodpłatnej pomocy prawnej – beneficjenci regulacji ustawowej*, „Studia Iuridica Lublinensia" 2016, nr XXV(3), pp. 867–879.

8 Winczorek, *Pandemia COVID-19*, pp. 38–61.

9 Konstytucja Rzeczypospolitej Polskiej z 2 kwietnia 1997 r. (Dz.U. Nr 78, poz. 483 ze zm.); hereinafter „Konstytucja RP".

10 Winczorek, *Pandemia COVID-19*, p. 38.

11 Winczorek, *Pandemia COVID-19*, p. 40.

12 More: B. Przywora, *Normatywny*, pp. 163–224.

its source in human dignity). The jurisprudence of the Constitutional Tribunal emphasised: "The problem of legal aid for the poor has a constitutional rank, as well as a rank resulting from the international standards of human rights protection binding on Poland. It does not apply only to criminal cases, but to all cases heard by the courts."[13]

In creating a system of free pre-litigation legal aid, the following constitutional norms should be taken into account in particular:

(a) The principle of social justice (Article 2 of the Constitution of the Republic of Poland), having an anchor in human dignity ordering the state to provide assistance wherever human dignity is threatened or violated (Article 30 of the Constitution of the Republic of Poland);
(b) The principle of equal treatment (Article 32 of the Polish Constitution);
(c) The principle of the right to defence (Articles 42(2), 45(1) and (2), 77(2), 78); and
(d) The principle of protection of (equal) freedoms and rights of man and citizen (Chapter II of the Polish Constitution, including Article 80 of the Polish Constitution).

The state, creating a system of free pre-litigation legal aid, should take into account regulations of a social nature, concerning:

1. Persons with disabilities (Article 69 of the Polish Constitution); and
2. protection:
   (a) Family (Articles 18 and 71(1) of the Polish Constitution);
   (b) Maternity (Articles 18 and 71(2) of the Polish Constitution);
   (c) The rights of the child (Article 72 of the Polish Constitution);
   (d) The rights of consumers, users, and tenants against activities that threaten their health, privacy, and safety, and against unfair market practices (Article 76 of the Polish Constitution); and
   (e) veterans of the struggle for independence, especially invalids of war (Article 19 of the Polish Constitution).[14]

---

13 Judgment of the Constitutional Court from 29.08. 2006 r., SK 23/05, OTK-A 2006, nr 8, poz. 94.

14 See also: Przywora, *Normatywny*, pp. 243–261.

Thus, from the Constitution of the Republic of Poland comes the protection of a weaker individual in a difficult life situation[15] (a positive obligation[16]). This can take place within the framework of the system of legal aid, as it is broadly understood, while maintaining the norms of the Constitution of the Republic of Poland (including, in particular, the principle of equality and non-discrimination on any grounds). Such reasoning was also derived by the Constitutional Tribunal. In the opinion of the Constitutional Tribunal: state assistance to a party who is unable to bear the costs of professional legal aid is important to ensure the realisation of the right to a fair hearing by the court (Article 45 paragraph 1 of the Constitution). Legal aid under the norms of the Constitution of the Republic of Poland can also be read as an element of the realisation of the right to social security arising from (Article 67 of the Constitution of the Republic of Poland). The Court itself stressed: "The problem of legal aid for the poor has a constitutional rank, as well as a rank arising from international standards of human rights protection binding on Poland. This does not apply only to criminal cases, but to all cases heard by the courts."[17]

3.2. Material scope of the concept of free pre-litigation legal aid

From the point of view of the scope of the Law on Free Legal Aid, the following concepts should be considered:

---

15 See Jan Paweł II, *Nauczanie społeczne*, t. 3, Warszawa 1984, p. 165; Lipowicz, *O mądre*, pp. 314–315; M. Florczak-Wątor, *Podstawy prawne obowiązków ochronnych państwa w Konstytucji RP*, [in:] *Ochrona praw człowieka. Zagadnienia praktyczne*, red. A. Hauser, M. Urbaniak, Poznań 2019, p. 41; J. Czepek, *Zobowiązania pozytywne państwa w sferze praw człowieka pierwszej generacji na tle Europejskiej Konwencji Praw Człowieka*, Olsztyn 2014, pp. 21–26; S. Nitecki, *Solidarność a pomoc społeczna*, [in:] *Państwo solidarne*, red. A. Łabno, Warszawa 2018, p. 186; M. Florczak-Wątor, *Horyzontalny wymiar praw konstytucyjnych*, Kraków 2014. See also judgment of the Constitutional Court from 31.07. 2015 r., K 41/12, OTK-A 2015, nr 7, poz. 102.

16 More on this topic, e.g. C. Mik, *Teoria obowiązków pozytywnych państw-stron traktatów w dziedzinie praw człowieka na przykładzie Europejskiej Konwencji Praw Człowieka*, [in:] *Księga Jubileuszowa Profesora Tadeusza Jasudowicza*, red. J. Białocerkiewicz, M. Balcerzak, A. Czeczko-Durlak, Toruń 2004, pp. 257–276; E. H. Morawska, *Zobowiązania pozytywne państw-stron Konwencji o ochronie praw człowieka i podstawowych wolności*, Warszawa 2016.

17 Judgment of the Constitutional Court from 29.08. 2006 r., SK 23/05.

(a) free legal aid;
(b) free civic counselling;
(c) free legal education; and
(d) free mediation.[18]

The analysis of the norms leads to the conclusion that free pre-litigation legal aid includes several elements. On the one hand, it boils down to informing an individual about the applicable legal status and the rights or obligations to which he is entitled, including in connection with pending proceedings (preparatory, administrative, judicial or administrative court proceedings), on the other hand, alternatively, the possibility of indicating to an entitled person how to solve his legal problem or drafting a letter in the above-mentioned matters is allowed, excluding pleadings in pending proceedings (preparatory or judicial and letters in pending administrative court proceedings). Finally, free legal aid includes free mediation or drafting a letter for exemption from court costs or appointment of an ex officio attorney in court proceedings or appointment of an attorney, legal counsel, tax advisor or patent agent in administrative court proceedings, as well as informing the party about the costs of the proceedings and the financial risks associated with taking the case to court (Article 3 of the LFLA).

The expansion of the scope of the law's subject matter to include the possibility of informing an individual of the applicable legal status and his or her rights or obligations, including in connection with pending pre-trial, administrative, judicial or administrative proceedings, should be viewed positively. In addition, the introduced normalisation amounting to drafting a letter, but excluding pleadings in pending pre-trial or judicial proceedings and letters in pending administrative court proceedings, should be viewed positively. The adopted solution makes it possible to draft, for example, a lawsuit, as it is not a letter "in pending proceedings", but only initiates these proceedings. From the practice of providing free legal aid, one can point to the problem of the technical limitations in drafting such a pleading, initiating court proceedings during a single duty (four hours).[19] Despite the fact that several years have already passed, these issues are still unresolved and need to be clarified in order to avoid misunderstandings and to ensure

---

18 See e.g. M. Jabłoński, Prawo *do nieodpłatnej pomocy prawnej jako „element treści konstytucyjnego prawa do sądu" – uwagi na te postanowień ustawy z 5 sierpnia 2015 r. o nieodpłatnej pomocy prawnej oraz edukacji prawnej*, [in:] *Ochrona praw człowieka. Zagadnienia praktyczne*, red. A. Hauser, M. Urbaniak, Poznań 2019, pp. 96–100; zob. też np. Przywora and Wróbel, *Poradnictwo*, pp. 9–12.

19 Compare Płażek, *Nowe*, p. 299.

a proper standard for the provision of free legal aid. In addition, the drafting of a letter does not apply to letters in pending preliminary or judicial proceedings and letters in pending administrative court proceedings. This solution should be evaluated positively, taking into account the circumstance that an individual at the judicial stage is entitled to a defence counsel (attorney) ex officio – under the terms of the law.

In the practice of providing this public service, it is also a difficult problem to determine the precise understanding under the law in question – the meaning of assistance in drafting a pleading? It seems that this concept includes, on the one hand, the correction of the text drafted by the authorised person, and on the other hand, the dictation of the letter or the drafting of the letter by a lawyer in its entirety. The exclusion of the preparation of letters filed in pending pre-trial, judicial or administrative court proceedings means that the scope of legal aid includes the preparation of only letters initiating the indicated proceedings and letters in administrative proceedings.[20]

Within the framework of the Law on Free Legal Aid, it is possible to provide the entitled person with information as to the type of letter, or to indicate the remedy, as well as to inform him about the legal consequences of launching a legal action and the chances of success. However, it is debatable whether, within the framework of the public service of free pre-litigation legal aid, it is permissible to assess the merits of the letter of the eligible person's litigation opponent and submit a letter proposal to him. Some justification for such action is provided by the rules of ethics of the legal profession, which provide for the performance of legal services without remuneration.[21] This is a special kind of relationship linking a client (beneficiary of assistance) with an advocate (legal counsel) within the meaning of the provisions of the Law of 26 May 1982 – Law on Advocates[22] and the Law of 6 July 1982 on Legal Advisors.[23] However, what remains debatable is the handling of such a case by an advocate (legal advisor) after exhaustion of the activities of free assistance.[24]

A further question is how the relationship should be established between free legal aid and the so-called "free civic counselling", which involves activities

20 See J. Wegner, B. Wróblewski, *Prawo jednostki do nieodpłatnej pomocy prawnej*, „Przegląd Prawa Publicznego" 2021, nr 6, pp. 9–10.

21 See Wegner and Wróblewski, *Prawo*, p. 10.

22 Tekst jedn. Dz. U. z 2022 r. poz. 1184 z późn. zm.; dalej: „pr. adw.".

23 Tekst jedn. Dz.U. z 2022 r. poz. 1166; dalej: „u.r.p.".

24 See also: Wegner and Wróblewski, *Prawo*, p. 10.

tailored to the individual situation of the person entitled, with the aim of raising awareness of his or her rights or obligations. The legislator uses the indefinite term "civic counselling", which raises problems of interpretation in distinguishing activities tailored to the individual situation of the entitled person from activities undertaken in the course of providing free legal aid. Justifiably, the case law emphasises:

> The statutory definition of civic counselling indicates the forms of activities that the legislator has defined as activities tailored to the individual situation of the entitled person, aimed at raising the awareness of this person about his/her rights or obligations, and indicates the possibility of drawing up an action plan together with the entitled person and assistance in its implementation.

The law only lists examples of activities under this counselling. These are activities of a supportive nature, such as advice for people in debt, advice on housing issues and social security. Thus, the catalogue is open, as supported by the construction of the provision. One should agree with the position, "Civic counselling is not limited to legal actions, but makes it possible to advise certain factual actions in addition to or instead of legal actions."[25] Irrespective of this, however, there is no doubt that in both cases it may be applicable to inform an individual of the pertaining legal state of affairs and the rights to which he is entitled or the obligations incumbent upon him (Article 3.1.1 LFLA). Already a cursory analysis of Articles 3 and 3a of the Law on Free Legal Aid provides grounds for the conclusion that, although free civic counselling does not have to be limited exclusively to legal activities, legal advice may be part of it.[26] Besides, it is difficult to imagine that a person providing assistance with regard to incurring an obligation (e.g. a loan), or applying for compensation or an estate or separation would not refer to the law. Several years of practice in the civic counselling system leads to such conclusions. The implementation of this counselling mostly boils down to the provision of legal assistance in various dimensions. If so, it does not justify the differentiation of free legal aid from civic counselling. Moreover, the implementation of civic counselling – support in solving a problem on one's own by the beneficiary – remains highly debatable, since it largely boils down to the provision of legal assistance, and often to the preparation of a draft letter. The

---

25 Wyrok WSA w Warszawie z 04.05.2021 r., VII SA/Wa 2268/20, LEX nr 3265719.

26 Hałub-Kowalczyk, *Sformalizowany*, p. 183; D. Daniluk, *Nieodpłatne poradnictwo obywatelskie w świetle ustawy o nieodpłatnej pomocy prawnej, nieodpłatnym poradnictwie obywatelskim oraz edukacji prawnej. Wymiar teoretyczny i praktyczny*, „Przegląd Prawa Publicznego" 2022, nr 10, pp. 44–45.

question arises whether this is a form of empowerment for the eligible party, or rather a dereliction of his independent action?[27]

The lack of a precise definition of this concept and the criteria for verification does not lead to the conclusion that an efficient system of free legal aid is in place. Moreover, taking into account the requirements for persons to carry out this task (the so-called advisors), it leads to a lowering of standards in the legal security of citizens.[28] The requirements placed on advisors significantly deviate from the standards that provide a guarantee of reliable performance of citizens' advice, expected of a person providing legal advice. A 70-hour course in citizenship counselling, of which at least 15 hours shall be devoted to classes on the methodology of the counsellor's work and at least 20 hours shall be devoted to classes on debt counselling, has been stipulated as sufficient to provide assistance in the form of civic counselling. In addition, the counsellor is required to attend a refresher course at least once a year, starting from the year following the year in which he completed the training or obtained a certificate. In adopting this normalisation, the legislator should have been aware of the decline in the quality-of-service provision in the area of civic counselling.[29] It remains highly questionable whether a person who is not a professional attorney (lawyer or counsellor), who completes the training, is able to effectively and with due professionalism provide a service that includes, in particular, advice: 1) to people in debt; 2) on housing issues; and 3) on social security. This often requires not only the specialisation of the lawyer (legal counsel), but also the possession of relevant experience in this area. In our opinion, there is no rational argument for the introduction of so-called advisors into the legal aid system. This too does not show evidence of a well-thought-out concept for building a free legal aid system.

Another problem for the legislator with regard to free civic counselling is the issue of drafting letters. It follows from Article 3a of the Law on Free Legal Aid that free civic counselling includes activities tailored to the individual situation of the entitled person, aimed at raising the person's awareness of his or her rights or obligations and support in solving the problem independently. Thus, various activities fall within the scope of this provision, including, as the provision states, "if necessary, drawing up a plan of action together with the authorised person

27 Daniluk, *Nieodpłatne poradnictwo*, p. 53.

28 Uchwała nr 79/2018 Prezydium Naczelnej Rady Adwokackiej z 19 czerwca 2018 r., p. 1; source: http://www.adwokatura.pl/admin/wgrane_pliki/file-uchwala-nr-79-2018-23655.pdf (access: 28.06.2022 r.).

29 Uchwała nr 79/2018 Prezydium Naczelnej Rady Adwokackiej z 19 czerwca 2018 r., p. 1.

and assistance in its implementation." The question arises whether assistance in implementing the plan of action does not include assistance in drawing up a letter, for example, in matters of indebtedness, or in the field of housing and social security issues? In our opinion, this cannot be excluded. The provision only implies the possibility of drawing up an action plan, but there are no guidelines on what it consists of and in what form it should be drawn up. Thus, it can be interdisciplinary and focused on social activation.[30] What's more, free civic counselling also includes free mediation (Article 3(2) LFLA). Free mediation, on the other hand, includes:

1. informing the entitled person about the possibilities of using amicable methods of dispute resolution, in particular mediation, and the benefits of doing so;
2. preparation of a draft mediation agreement or request for mediation;
3. preparation of a draft request for mediation in a criminal case;
4. conducting mediation; and
5. providing assistance in drafting an application to the court for approval of a settlement reached before a mediator (Article 4a LFLA).

With this in mind, it is worth considering simplifying these legal regulations and placing counselling within the framework of free pre-litigation legal aid.

At the same time as introducing civic counselling, the legislator created a new category of persons to handle this task – the so-called advisors. However, the requirements for advisors significantly deviate from the standards that are a guarantee of reliable performance of civic counselling. The lack of a precise definition of this concept and appropriate regulations to guarantee the reliability of the task will lead to a lowering of standards of legal security.[31]

Other forms of implementation of the legal advice system can also be seen in Poland. For example, specialised counselling (in particular, legal, psychological and family counselling), is provided to individuals and families having difficulties or showing the need for support in solving their life problems, regardless of their income (Article 46(1)) stems from the Act of 12 March 2004 on social assistance.[32] The purpose is to provide individuals and families with support in difficult, crisis situations. Assistance is reduced to providing information, advice, and indication of specialised support institutions or administrative offices for

30 See also: Hałub-Kowalczyk, *Formalized*, pp. 182–183.
31 Uchwała nr 79/2018 Prezydium Naczelnej Rady Adwokackiej z 19 czerwca 2018 r., p. 1.
32 Tekst jedn. Dz.U. z 2021 r. poz. 2268 ze zm.; hereinafter: „u.p.s.".

handling specific matters. This counselling is within the framework of specific activities undertaken by professional counsellors and persons assisting individuals who are in difficult situations.

In addition, specialised counselling is carried out as part of the poviat's own tasks (Art. 19 pt. 2 of the Act)[33]; it follows from the Act of 8 March 1990 on municipal self-government[34] that the poviat's tasks include, in particular, matters of "pro-family policy, including the provision of social, medical and legal care for pregnant women" (Art. 7 para. 1 pt. 16),[35] and from the Act of 26 October 1982 on Upbringing in Sobriety and Counteracting Alcoholism[36] which stipulates that government administration and local government bodies "also support the establishment and development of social organisations whose purpose is to promote sobriety and abstinence, influence alcohol abusers and provide assistance to their families, as well as provide conditions conducive to the activities of such organizations" (Article 1(2)).[37]

In Poland, the institution of counselling also appears in other laws. For example, in Article 46 of the Law on Social Welfare, specialised counselling is broadly defined as legal, psychological and family counselling, provided to individuals and families having difficulties or demonstrating the need for support in solving their life problems, regardless of their income (paragraph 1), and the tasks of the district include the provision of specialised counselling (Article 19, point 2 of the Law on Social Welfare).[38]

---

33 The legislation adopted a solution that poviats play a complementary function to communes to some extent. Hence, they were entrusted with local tasks that the communes are unable to cope with. The rationale of this solution was that the poviat has greater economic, financial and organizational potential than the commune, and can independently perform tasks with a higher degree of complexity or specialization. Hence, the poviat is a centre gathering basic institutions providing specialized services to the inhabitants of individual communes; W. Maciejko, [in:] W. Maciejko, P. Zaborniak, *Ustawa o pomocy społecznej. Komentarz*, Warszawa 2013, LEX, komentarz do art. 19 u.p.s.

34 Tekst jedn. Dz.U. z 2022 r. poz. 559 ze zm.

35 For more see on the tasks of the commune: M. Augustyniak, T. Moll [in:] *Ustawa o samorządzie gminnym. Komentarz*, red. B. Dolnicki, Warszawa 2021, LEX, commentary on art. 7.

36 Tekst jedn. Dz.U. z 2021 r. poz. 1119 ze zm.

37 See also I. Niżnik-Dobosz, [in:] M. Koszowski, I. Niżnik-Dobosz, *Ustawa o wychowaniu w trzeźwości i przeciwdziałaniu alkoholizmowi. Komentarz*, Warszawa 2020.

38 See also: WSA w Poznaniu z 19 października 2017 r., II SAB/Po 47/16, LEX nr 2424828.

One can also point to the legal advice provided in the exercise of the mandate of MP and senator. However, it is fundamental that the provision of legal advice in the parliamentarian's office is related to the exercise of the rights and duties of parliamentarians (arising from Articles 19–24 of the Law of 9 May 1996 on the Exercise of the Mandate of Member of Parliament and Senator[39]). The activities of the parliamentarian's office can be financed from funds allocated for the operation of parliamentary (senatorial) offices. It is reasonable to delineate the framework for the provision of such legal assistance in the offices of parliamentarians and to clarify the catalogue of persons who can provide such assistance. This assistance is organised in different ways. It can be provided both by office staff (it also cannot exclude people without legal education and qualifications) and volunteers (usually students or graduates of law faculties).

3.3. Subjective scope

Free legal aid (or free civic counselling) is available to an eligible person who is unable to bear the costs of paid legal aid, including an individual who is a sole proprietor who has not employed others in the past year. Provided as a requirement, before obtaining this public service, is the obligation of the eligible person to submit a written statement that he or she is unable to bear the costs of paid legal aid, and a person receiving free legal aid or free civic counselling in the scope of his or her business activities shall additionally submit a statement that he or she has not employed other persons during the past year (Article 4 LFLA).

This is a far-reaching change from the solutions under the 2015 Law on Free Legal Aid in its original form. The change was determined by the low interest in obtaining free legal aid, while funding the willingness to provide this assistance.[40] While the idea of expanding the catalogue of persons entitled to benefit from the public service (the so-called beneficiaries) gained recognition among

---

39 Tekst jedn. Dz.U. z 2022 r. poz. 1339; see in the literature, especially with regard to the obligation of government and local government administration bodies to provide assistance to parliamentarians in the performance of their functions: P. J. Uziębło, [in:] K. Grajewski, J. Stelina, P. J. Uziębło, *Komentarz do ustawy o wykonywaniu mandatu posła i senatora*, Warszawa 2014, LEX, komentarz do art. 24; B. Przywora, *Z problematyki wykonywania mandatu posła i senatora – kilka refleksji*, [in:] *Ustroje – prawa człowieka – bezpieczeństwo – integracja europejska. Księga Jubileuszowa z okazji 70 urodzin Profesora Jerzego Jaskierni*, red. R. M. Czarny, Ł. Baratyński, P. Ramiączek, K. Spryszak, t. 1, Toruń 2020, pp. 160–170.

40 Informacja NIK…, p. 21.

practitioners, experts, NGOs, as well as independent bodies (the Ombudsman), the final statutory solution already raises doubts. This is because a broad formula was adopted without specifying any criteria. Only the following statement is required: "free legal aid and free civic counselling shall be available to an eligible person who is unable to bear the costs of paid legal aid". Thus, an individual, wishing to use this public service, is obliged to make a statement to the person providing free legal aid or free counselling. Such a solution will undoubtedly promote interest in this public service, as the state thus "opens" the system of free assistance to new beneficiaries. However, on the other hand, such a broad formulation of the provision provides room for abuse of this service. It is worth considering at least the introduction of a proviso that the person's statement is made under pain of criminal liability. The practice of providing this task also leads to such conclusions. The problem of the criterion for entitlement to free legal aid, which boils down to the submission of a statement, was pointed out in particular by the Presidium of the Supreme Bar Council, recognising that such a solution "paradoxically significantly restricts access to free legal aid, excluding people in a difficult financial situation who, however, can afford to pay the low costs of paid pre-litigation legal aid".[41] The point is that the state should conduct policy taking into account, in particular, the principle of a social market economy and the principle of social justice, as well as the rationalisation of public spending (especially in the face of a situation of economic crisis). In turn, this means that the state should first address free legal aid to those who really need it. Such mechanisms were also introduced by the legislature at the stage of judicial proceedings. While the state may decide to provide everyone with access to free legal aid or free Internet, the consequence of this is to guarantee the provision with the principle of equality and non-discrimination for any reason.[42]

Hence, as part of the rationalisation of public spending, the introduction of some objective criteria for access to this service should be considered. For example, one can point – referring to the Swedish solutions analysed herein – to the income criterion.[43] In Poland, there have also been proposals to introduce

41 Uchwała nr 79/2018 Prezydium Naczelnej Rady Adwokackiej z 19 czerwca 2018 r., p. 1.

42 Compare M. Florczak-Wątor, *Konstytucja jako źródło obowiązków państwa w stosunku do obywatela*, „Ruch Prawniczy, Ekonomiczny I Socjologiczny" 2018, t. 80, nr 1, p. 128.

43 The legislation of the Kingdom of Sweden has not adopted the notion of unpaid legal aid. The person is obliged to pay the appropriate amount depending on the value of the subject of the dispute. The percentage breakdown of the contribution is regulated as follows: (1) 2% if the value of legal aid does not exceed SEK 50,000; (2) 5%, but not less than SEK 500 if the value of the legal aid does not exceed SEK 100,000; (3) 10%,

this criterion (Presidium of the Supreme Council of Advocates,[44] Ombudsman,[45] recommendations of the First Congress of Civil Rights,[46] Presidium of the National Council of Legal Advisers[47]). We believe that the income criterion (without prejudging its amount, which requires taking into account a number of external factors subject to change), will make it possible to better realise the basic objective of the Law on free legal aid – that is, to guarantee access to free pre-litigation legal aid to persons who are unable to receive legal advice against payment. In turn, the introduced solutions allow any person who declares that he or she remains in such a situation to benefit from free legal aid.[48]

Other solutions may also be considered. For example, it seems reasonable to formally separate information from legal advice which, by the nature of the service, requires much more involvement (such as the first pleading in a case[49]).

---

but not less than SEK 1,000, if the value of the legal aid exceeds SEK 100,000 but does not exceed SEK 120,000; (4) 20% but not less than SEK 1,500 if the value of the legal aid exceeds SEK 120,000 but is not more than SEK 150,000; (5) 30% but not less than SEK 2,000 if the value of the legal aid exceeds SEK 150,000. but not higher than SEK 200,000.

44 Uchwała nr 79/2018 Prezydium Naczelnej Rady Adwokackiej z 19 czerwca 2018 r.

45 Informacja o stanie przestrzegania wolności i praw człowieka i obywatela w 2017 r. oraz o działalności Rzecznika Praw Obywatelskich, p. 168, source: https://bip.brpo.gov.pl/pl/content/informacja-o-stanie-przestrzegania-wolnosci-i-praw-czlowieka-i-obywatela-w-2017-r-oraz-o (access: 22.12.2022).

46 Załącznik nr 3 Rekomendacje I Kongresu Praw Obywatelskich: Rekomendacja pt. „Pomoc w trudnych sytuacjach, w tym pomoc prawna" zamieszczona w informacji o stanie przestrzegania wolności i praw człowieka i obywatela w 2017 r. oraz o działalności Rzecznika Praw Obywatelskich, p. 575.

47 Stanowisko Prezydium Krajowej Rady Radców Prawnych z 9 października 2017 r. w sprawie przedstawionej przez Prezydenta RP nowelizacji ustawy z 5 sierpnia 2015 r. o nieodpłatnej pomocy prawnej i edukacji prawnej (druk sejmowy nr 1868), s. 4, source: https://orka.sejm.gov.pl/Druki8ka.nsf/0/4A58B025E60CA65DC12581B50033C036/%24File/1868-001.pdf (access: 22.12.2022).

48 Compare Stanowisko Rzecznika Praw Obywatelskich zawarte w piśmie do Prezydenta RP w zakresie zakresu zmian w ustawie o nieodpłatnej pomocy prawnej: Pismo RPO IV.510.9.2014.AB, p. 3, source: https://bip.brpo.gov.pl/sites/default/files/Wyst%C4%85pienie%20do%20Prezydenta%20RP%20w%20sprawie%20nieodp%C5%82atnej%20pomocy%20prawnej.pdf (access: 22.12.2022 r.).

49 Proposals of the Institute of Public Affairs included in the final report on the monitoring of the functioning of the system of free legal aid, prepared under the Program „Wspieranie Organizacji Pozarządowych 2016 – Obywatel i Prawo" Polish-American Freedom Foundation implemented by the Institute of Public Affairs, p. 64; while NIK submits, among others, o taking action to "conduct an analysis of the possibility of

Deciding on such a separation, the legislator should consistently introduce a gradation of the free legal aid service into:

(a) basic free legal assistance; and
(b) qualified free legal assistance.[50]

With such a separation, it could be assumed that citizens would be guaranteed free access to obtain at least basic legal assistance regarding their rights and procedural options for asserting them before public authorities. In particular, remote mode communication mechanisms could be used in this regard, with the guarantee of highly qualified persons professionally trained to provide legal assistance (e.g. solicitors, legal advisors, tax advisors, patent attorneys or trainee solicitors or trainee legal advisors). Given the remote mode of such provision, it is easier to provide a specialised legal service. The advantage of such a solution would also be that the beneficiary would receive due (reliable) knowledge of the state of the case, his rights and possible solutions at the initial stage of the case. On this basis, a person could decide on the next steps of action.

The current solutions do not fully guarantee the due level of the service provided, as they allow the provision of legal assistance in centres operated by NGOs by persons who are not professional attorneys but have a legal education and at least three years of experience in performing activities requiring legal knowledge directly related to the provision of legal assistance. The question arises, what are the real possibilities for verifying the quality of the service provided and the responsibility of such a person for misinforming the beneficiary of the service? With this in mind, we believe that the proper entities to delegate persons to provide the service of free legal aid are, in particular, the district chambers of attorneys and legal advisers. These entities have reliable information about persons specialised in particular disciplines of law, and it is possible – for the purposes of the free legal aid service – to use this database. The adoption of such a solution would be important for several more reasons. On the one hand, it would serve to fully professionalise the service and, on the other, it would strengthen the level of trust of the beneficiaries of this service. There is another argument in favour of providing this service at the stage of basic free legal aid remotely.

---

implementing publicly available and non-individualized legal information, including the use of modern technologies" – see Informacja o wynikach kontroli, p. 23.

50 Compare: rządowy projekt ustawy o dostępie do nieodpłatnej pomocy prawnej przyznawanej przez państwo osobom fizycznym, Sejm V Kadencji, druk sejmowy nr 29, pp. 4–5. Source: http://orka.sejm.gov.pl/proc5.nsf/opisy/29.htm (access: 02.07.2022).

During the period of restrictions caused by the COVID-19 pandemic, medical advice services were also provided via electronic communication (as a rule, the so-called first contact visit[51]). Thus, it seems that the provision of the service of free legal aid may be all the more applicable in this regard. Moreover, by the Law of 14 May 2020 on amendments to certain laws on protective measures in connection with the spread of the SARS-CoV-2 virus[52] it was provided that in the event of a state of epidemic emergency, a state of epidemic or the introduction of a state of emergency, the provision of free legal aid or the provision of free civic counselling may be carried out by means of distance communication and off the premises of the centre. Thus, the legislator created the possibility for all citizens to receive free assistance advice remotely during the pandemic (using means of remote communication, i.e. telephone or instant messenger).[53]

As can be seen from the justification of the bill (Ninth Term/Parliament Print 344), the primary objectives of the package of laws called "Anti-Crisis Shield" were indicated as "preventing the negative effects of economic changes resulting from the COVID-19 pandemic", "not only mitigating the consequences – the direct effects of the epidemic, but also preparing both the Polish economy and administrative structures for the challenges that await our country after the outbreaks are extinguished". These provisions concerned the manner in which the district governors would perform the tasks referred to in the law on free legal aid in conditions of a declared state of epidemic emergency, a state of epidemic, as well as other extraordinary states related to the danger of spreading infection or contagious disease, which may threaten public health. The idea was to ensure the fulfilment of the public task under the conditions of the introduced ban on movement, the safety of the beneficiaries of assistance, the persons providing this assistance and the employees of the units where the centres of providing assistance were located, there is a need to specifically regulate the rules of providing assistance. The justification for the project assumes that the way of providing assistance under remote conditions should be based on the model for the implementation of this task concerning persons with significant

51 See Pismo Rzecznika Praw Obywatelskich, IV.510.9.2014.AB, p. 7.

52 Dz. U. 2020 poz. 875. Na podstawie art. 29 pkt 7 wprowadzono 28a do ustawy z dnia 5 sierpnia 2015 r. o nieodpłatnej pomocy prawnej, nieodpłatnym poradnictwie obywatelskim oraz edukacji prawnej (Dz. U. z 2019 r. poz. 294).

53 D. Daniluk, Zmiany regulacji prawnych dotyczących nieodpłatnej pomocy prawnej i nieodpłatnego poradnictwa obywatelskiego w związku z pandemią wirusa SARS-CoV-2 „Przegląd Legislacyjny" 2022/1, p. 140.

motor disabilities who cannot appear at the centre in person, as well as persons experiencing communication difficulties, as referred to in the Act of 19 August 2011 on Sign Language and Other Means of Communication[54] (i.e. according to the principles regulated in § 4 of the Ordinance of the Minister of Justice of 21 December 2018 on free legal aid and free civic counselling).[55] The idea of remote provision of assistance as a permanent possibility was also considered within the framework of the work of the Ministry of Justice, with – according to the 2020 report – the choice of form being up to the beneficiary of the assistance. This would apply not only to the epidemic period. One should agree with the statement that this solution "worked well during the difficult time of the pandemic and its continuation is expected by society", and as an additional effect is indicated "the abolition of regionalisation, reducing the burden on the most beleaguered points, and adding work to the least effective ones".[56] A positive picture of the remote mode of providing free assistance also emerges from the Ministry of Justice's 2021 report. The report cites the results of non-standard service delivery channels, indicating that the search for innovations in this area can help increase the efficiency of legal aid. The Justice Ministry reports that in 2021 "in 171,526 cases, assistance was provided by telephone"[57] and states that "supporting standard forms of assistance provision (the so-called stationary mode) by a non-standard one (the so-called remote mode), as well as facilitating access to the latter without having to meet the prerequisites of Article 28a of the Law, can be of great benefit to beneficiaries of legal aid".[58] The indicated arguments provide a basis for recommending the provision of basic free pre-litigation legal aid remotely. Optimisation of the system of free legal aid should be indicated as the *ratio of* such a solution.

Based on the above findings, we propose basic free pre-litigation legal assistance. In essence, this would be the first meeting of the beneficiary of the service with a person with qualified powers of representation (e.g. lawyer, legal counsel, notary, tax advisor). The purpose of this meeting would be to determine the legal problem, notify about rights and obligations, and the procedure for action (e.g. referral to an appropriate public entity, or to provide assistance within the

---

54 Dz. U. z 2017 r. poz. 1824.
55 Dz. U. poz. 2492.
56 Ocena Ministra Sprawiedliwości za 2020 r., p. 41.
57 Ocena Ministra Sprawiedliwości za 2021 r., p. 39.
58 Ocena Ministra Sprawiedliwości za 2021 r., p. 39.

possibilities provided by the law: i.e. free legal aid, free civic counselling or free mediation).

The beneficiaries of the basic service of free legal aid (legal information) would be all interested citizens, or even all persons residing on the territory of the Republic of Poland. However, this assistance would be limited only to providing information on the current legal status and the rights and obligations arising therefrom. Such a solution would be more useful from the point of view of economic analysis of the law, for with the same organisational costs it will to a greater extent at the basic level allow the right to a court and the principle of social justice. All the more so, since the process of providing free legal aid at this level can lead to greater involvement of, for example, trainee attorneys and counsellors. According to the National Council of the Judiciary:

> the involvement of qualified lawyers should be evaluated positively, however, limiting ourselves only to advocates and legal advisers is the most expensive and inefficient solution. This is because the solutions operating in the world focus on organizing the system in such a way that the cases that require it go to the attorneys, and others are solved by qualified counsel.[59]

The idea is that a structured system of free legal aid at the pre-litigation stage should be (as a last resort) a bridge to the effective assertion of rights at the court stage.

In addition to completely free basic free pre-litigation legal aid, we propose qualified (advanced) legal aid for beneficiaries. We believe that it is necessary in this case to introduce restrictions on access. Namely, in our view, this assistance should in particular be addressed to persons who are:

1. benefiting from:
   (a) societal,
   (b) family,
   (c) pensions,
   (d) or social benefits;
2. unemployed;
3. disabled;
4. from single-parent and disadvantaged families;
5. affected by domestic violence;

---

59 Opinia Krajowej Rady Sądownictwa z 16.01.2015 r. w przedmiocie projektu ustawy o nieodpłatnej pomocy prawnej i informacji prawnej, pp. 1–2, source https://www.adwokatura.pl/admin/wgrane_pliki/file-opiniakrspomoc-10974.pdf (access: 22.12.2022 r.).

6. endangered by:
   (a) demoralisation,
   (b) or exploitation;
7. crime victims;
8. those with low material status (verified by income criteria);
9. non-Polish nationals;
10. minors;
11. prison inmates;
12. affected by an unforeseen event (such as a natural disaster);
13. individuals launching the operation of a business;
14. veterans of the struggle for independence, especially war invalids;
15. refugees; and
16. those against whom reprivatisation proceedings are pending provided that the income criterion is met.[60]

The argument in favour of this proposal consists in protecting in a special way people who are in a difficult financial and living situation. The case for providing free legal aid to these people is supported directly or indirectly on the one hand, by international norms, and on the other hand, by constitutional provisions (in particular, the principle of social justice, which finds its source in human dignity, or regulations on protective rights and obligations, which boil down to public authorities taking action aimed at protecting the weaker individual). In our proposal, free qualified legal aid at the pre-litigation stage would include, in particular:

(a) analysis of documentation and verification of the proposal for a solution resulting from the meeting within the framework of basic free legal aid;
(b) assistance to beneficiaries in preparing a draft of the first pleading;
(c) conducting pre-litigation mediation; and
(d) assistance – if necessary – in completing the application for appointment of an attorney ex officio and exemption from court costs.

The implementation of this type of assistance requires special commitment, as often the first letter to the court is the most important from the point of view

60 Compare propozycje Najwyższej Izby Kontroli (zawarte w Informacji o wynikach kontroli, s. 21) oraz Rzecznika Praw Obywatelskich (zawarte w Informacji o działalności Rzecznika Praw Obywatelskich w roku 2017, p. 168, source: https://www.rpo.gov.pl/sites/default/files/Informacja%20roczna%20RPO%20za%20rok%202017.pdf, (access: 22.12.2022).

of asserting rights. Thus, with a view to guaranteeing the proper level of professionalism with regard to a complex matter, this should be provided by highly qualified persons – lawyers and legal advisors. At this stage in the provision of legal aid, it is also reasonable to impose an obligation on the provider to advise about the costs of the proceedings and the financial risks associated with taking the case to court. This solution is on the basis of the Law on Free Legal Aid, but with the proposed separation of assistance into basic and qualified assistance, the addition of such an obligation seems particularly necessary. This is because in a lot of instances the analysis of all the documentation and a fair presentation of the case to the person concerned (including the costs of legal proceedings) determines his final decision to initiate legal proceedings or to abandon this action. All the more so since the beneficiary often provides materials relevant to the course of the case while preparing the pleading. The beneficiary, when entering into litigation, should be aware of the consequences arising from the rules of court proceedings, especially the associated financial risks, such as incurring the costs of legal representation of the party opposing the proceedings – in the event the case is resolved in its favour.

3.4. Task organisation

In Poland, the public task of providing free legal aid, free civic counselling and legal education are tasks assigned by the government administration, carried out by the poviat in agreement with municipalities or independently (Art. 8 (1) LFLA). The law on free legal aid specifies the organisation of the points of free legal aid and free civic counselling (Art. 11 LFLA). The basic principle adopted is that the poviat entrusts half of the centres to be run by advocates and legal advisers for the purpose of providing free legal aid, and half to a non-governmental organisation conducting public benefit activities for the purpose of providing free legal aid or free civic counselling.

Non-governmental organisations play an important role in Poland. The basic normative act defining their status is the Act of 24 April 2003 on public benefit activity and voluntary work.[61] This law regulates the following issues:

1. conduct of public benefit activities by NGOs in the sphere of public tasks, cooperation of public administration bodies with NGOs;
2. acquisition of public benefit organisation status by NGOs and the operation of public benefit organisations;

---

61 (t.j. Dz. U. z 2022 r. poz. 1327 z późn. zm.).

3. exercise of supervision over the conduct of public benefit activities;
4. creation and operation of public benefit activity councils; and
5. conditions for the performance of services by volunteers and the use of such services (Article 1).[62]

In legal terms, public benefit activity means socially useful activities carried out by non-governmental organisations in the area of fulfilment of public tasks. Thus, the criterion of public benefit activity, which determines the scope of the subject matter of these organisations, is important. The normative treatment of NGOs deserves attention primarily for two reasons. The separate legal nature of NGOs from units of the public finance sector should be emphasised. Under the law, the concept of a non-governmental organisation consists of many elements. The basic elements determining the nature of these entities include: the form of organisational separation, resulting in their location outside units belonging to the public finance sector; their non-profit character; and the purpose of their activities (Article 3 paragraph 2 of the APBAV).[63] The sphere of public tasks includes, in particular, tasks in the fields of:

1. social assistance;
2. family support and the foster care system;
3. creating conditions for meeting the housing needs of the local community;
4. providing free legal assistance and raising the public's legal awareness;
5. activities for the integration and reintegration of people at risk of social exclusion;
6. charitable activities; and
7. upholding and disseminating the national tradition, cultivating Polishness and developing national, civic and cultural awareness.[64]

---

62 See also: P. Staszczyk, Art. 1. [in:] *Ustawa o działalności pożytku publicznego i o wolontariacie. Komentarz*, Warszawa 2022; J. Blicharz, Art. 1 [in:] *Komentarz do ustawy o działalności pożytku publicznego i wolontariacie*, [in:] *Ustawa o działalności pożytku publicznego i wolontariacie. Ustawa o spółdzielniach socjalnych. Komentarz*, Warszawa 2012, art. 3.

63 J. Blicharz [in:] *Komentarz do ustawy o działalności pożytku publicznego i wolontariacie*, [in:] *Ustawa o działalności pożytku publicznego i wolontariacie. Ustawa o spółdzielniach socjalnych. Komentarz*, Warszawa 2012, art. 3.

64 M. Michalski, A. Kotowski, R. Wiśniewski, J. Dąbrowska, A. Syryt, M. Zarzecki, *Normatywny model współpracy samorządu terytorialnego z organizacjami pozarządowymi. Wybrane zagadnienia*, red. A. Kotowski, S. Wijas, Warszawa 2021, pp. 31–32.

From the point of view of the subject of the study, the entrustment of a public task by local government units is important. This can take place on various legal bases, in particular, by way of awarding a public contract under the Public Procurement Law or ordering the implementation of a task and financing it or subsidising it in the form of a grant. A unit of the public finance sector exercises control over the implementation of the entrusted public task and evaluates its implementation. Funds transferred to subsidise the implementation of a public task are public funds, subject to the regime of the Law on Public Finance and the Law on Violation of Public Finance Discipline.[65]

Pursuant to the first sentence of Article 13 (1) of the Law on Public Benefit Activity and Voluntary Work – a public administration body intending to commission the implementation of a public task to non-governmental organisations or entities listed in Article 3 (3), announces an open tender – a dilemma arises as to whether the poviat may also entrust the running of half of the free legal assistance centres to the entities listed in Article 3 (3) of the Law on Public Benefit Activity and Voluntary Work. According to Article 3(3) of this Act, public benefit and voluntary activities may also be carried out by:

- legal persons and organisational units acting on the basis of regulations on the relationship of the State to the Catholic Church in the Republic of Poland, on the relationship of the State to other churches and religious associations and on guarantees of freedom of conscience and religion, if their statutory objectives include conducting public benefit activities;
- associations of local government units;
- social cooperatives; and
- joint-stock companies and limited liability companies, as well as sports clubs that are companies operating on the basis of the provisions of the Sports Act of 25 June 2010 (Journal of Laws of 2014, item 715), which do not operate for profit and allocate their entire income to the realisation of their statutory objectives and do not allocate their profit for distribution among their shareholders, stockholders and employees.[66]

Entities authorised to provide free legal aid are, in addition to attorneys and legal advisors, non-governmental organisations conducting public benefit activities. Such legitimacy is provided by Art. 11 (1) of the LFLA. On the basis of this, the poviat is obliged to entrust the running of half of the free legal aid centres

65 Michalski et al., *Normatywny*, p. 48.

66 See also: Michalski et al., *Normatywny*, pp. 58–59.

to a non-governmental organisation conducting public benefit activities. This solution is a manifestation of the evaluation of the previous activities of these organisations in providing free legal assistance, while on the other hand, it allows them to provide free legal assistance under the rules set forth in the Act on free legal assistance. It follows from the Law on Free Legal Aid that if there are two centres per poviat, then:

1. attorneys or legal advisors are entrusted with running a single centre; and
2. the operation of the other is entrusted to a non-governmental organisation that provides free legal aid and free civic counselling at the centre for the time period indicated in the contract.

If there are three centres per poviat, then:

1. a non-governmental organisation shall be entrusted with the operation of two centres (with one allocated for the provision of free legal aid); and
2. a second centre for the provision of free civic counselling.

Another rule is that half of the centres to be run by a non-governmental organisation shall be allocated for the provision of free civic counselling. If the number of centres to be run by a non-governmental organisation is an odd number, the higher number of centres by one shall be allocated to the provision of free civic counselling, with the lower number of centres allocated to the provision of free legal aid. Depending on the needs of the local community, the district governor may, with the approval of the governor, within the number of centres to be run by a non-governmental organisation, allocate a larger number of centres for the provision of free civic counselling.[67]

From the point of view of the implementation of this task by a non-governmental organisation, the requirements of Article 11d of the Act are important. The provincial governor maintains a list of non-governmental organisations authorised to run centres for free legal aid, centres for free civic counselling and centres for free mediation in the province. Entry onto this list, in terms of providing free legal aid, may be applied for by a non-governmental organisation that jointly meets the following conditions:

1. it has at least two years' experience in performing tasks involving the provision of legal advice, legal information or citizenship counselling;

67 See also Daniluk, *Free counselling*, pp. 45–46.

2. it has a contract with an attorney, legal counsellor, tax advisor or person referred to in Article 11, paragraph 3, item 2, and a mediator;
3. it provides a guarantee of proper performance of the task, in particular, in terms of ensuring:
   (a) confidentiality in connection with the provision of free legal assistance and its documentation,
   (b) professional and reliable provision of free legal assistance,
   (c) adherence to the principles of ethics in the provision of free legal assistance, particularly when there is a conflict of interest; and
4. it has developed and applies service standards and an internal quality control system for the provision of free legal assistance.

According to Article 11d (3) of the Law, a non-governmental organisation that jointly meets the following conditions may apply for inclusion in the list referred to in paragraph 1 for the provision of free civic counselling:

1. it has at least two years' experience in tasks involving the provision of citizens' advice, acquired in the five years immediately preceding the submission of the application, or at least two years of experience in tasks involving the provision of legal advice, legal information or free counselling;
2. it has a contract with a consultant and mediator referred to in Article 4a (6);
3. it provides a guarantee of proper performance of the task, in particular in terms of ensuring:
   (a) confidentiality in connection with the provision of free civic counselling and its documentation,
   (b) professional and reliable provision of free civic counselling,
   (c) adherence to the principles of ethics in the provision of free civic counselling, especially when there is a conflict of interest; and
4. it has developed and applies service standards and an internal quality control system for the provision of free civic counselling.

Article 11d (2)-(3) of the Law on Free Legal Aid implies the positive prerequisites that should be met by a non-governmental organisation seeking to be included in the list for running free legal aid and free civic counselling centres. On the other hand, Article 11d (5) of the analysed law contains a negative premise, the occurrence of which makes it impossible for a non-governmental organisation to be included in the list maintained by the governor. Namely, a non-governmental organisation which, in the period of two years preceding the submission of the application, did not settle the grant awarded for the performance of a public task or used the grant inconsistently with the purpose for which it was awarded, as well as that non-governmental organisation with which the district governor has terminated the agreement, cannot apply for entry on the list. The two-year period runs from the date of accounting for the grant and returning the undue funds with interest, or termination of the agreement.[68]

Pursuant to Article 11d(12)(4) of the Act, the Governor shall issue a decision on deleting a non-governmental organisation from the list, with regard to providing free legal assistance, providing free civic counselling or conducting free mediation, in the event that the organisation has not provided a list or certificates. It should be emphasised here that the actions of the authority are mandatory, and the decision issued in this regard is binding. At the same time, the provisions of the cited law do not provide grounds for the authority to request supplementation of the submitted documentation. The obligation to comply with the statutory procedure with due diligence rests solely with the listed NGO.[69]

In order to verify that the listed non-governmental organisation meets the condition of professional and reliable provision of free civic counselling (Article 11d (3)(3)(b)), the governor evaluates selected counselling from the provision of free civic counselling at the centre. This evaluation is carried out in a way that guarantees its impartiality, based on the conclusions of a review by a counsellor who has a recommendation from an entity authorised to conduct training and refresher courses (Art. 11b (1) of the LFLA). The evaluation is forwarded by the provincial governor to the competent district governor. The advice, evaluation and review may be transmitted electronically.

The catalogue of entities authorised to provide legal assistance is closed. Pursuant to Article 5(1) of the LFLA, free legal aid is provided on the one hand personally by an advocate or legal adviser, and on the other hand, in particularly justified cases by their authorisation, by a trainee advocate or legal adviser. In addition, the law allows for the provision of legal assistance by a lawyer or tax advisor from a non-governmental organisation conducting public benefit activities (Art. 11 LFLA).[70] In legal aid centres entrusted to a non-governmental organisation, legal assistance may be also provided by:

1. a tax advisor – in the field of tax law, excluding business tax matters; and
2. a person who:

---

68 See also: Wyrok WSA w Warszawie z 26.04.2022 r., VII SA/Wa 2433/21, LEX nr 3407140.

69 See also: Wyrok WSA w Warszawie z 27.05.2021 r., VII SA/Wa 593/21, LEX nr 3194742.

70 See also: M. Kaczocha, *Ustawa o nieodpłatnej pomocy prawnej oraz edukacji prawnej. Komentarz*, LEX/el. 2016, Commentary on art. 11 u.n.p.p.

(a) completed higher legal studies and obtained a master's degree or foreign legal studies recognised in the Republic of Poland,
(b) has at least three years' experience in the performance of activities requiring legal knowledge directly related to the provision of legal assistance,
(c) enjoys full public rights and has full legal capacity, and
(d) has not been convicted of an intentional crime prosecuted by public indictment or a fiscal crime (Art. 11(3) of the LFLA).

The role of NGOs should be emphasised.

On the basis of Article 11(1), second sentence, of the law on legal aid, NGOs are statutorily guaranteed a 50% share in legal aid centres, which is why guarantees of high quality of advice provided by designated persons are so important. Taking into account such a broad catalogue of persons entitled to provide a free legal aid service (who are not necessarily professional attorneys), the problem arises of the quality of provision of this service by the persons performing this task, especially since the legislator should ensure that all citizens who cannot afford to obtain paid pre-litigation legal aid have the right to obtain legal aid provided at the highest possible level without discrimination.[71]

First, it follows from Article 7 (1) of the LFLA that there is an obligation to document each case of provision of free legal aid or free civic counselling on the free legal aid or free civic counselling assistance card. In particular, information on:

1. the reported case and the assistance provided;
2. the area of law to which the assistance was related;
3. case categories;
4. forms of assistance provided;
5. the time spent on it;
6. the number of visits by an authorised person to the same case; and
7. general information about the eligible person regarding, among other things: age, gender, education, income, household and place of residence, as well as data on the point, the person providing the assistance and the date it was provided.

The assistance card also includes a section covering the authorised person's opinion of the assistance provided. The authorised person's completion of this part of the assistance card (including providing a telephone number for further

71 Kaczocha, *Ustawa*, commentary on art. 11 u.n.p.p.

opinion), is subject to the authorised person's consent. It is important to note that the assistance card does not provide the authorised person's personal information, which can indisputably identify the person.[72]

Electronic documentation via an ICT system has been introduced, and the assistance card, which includes a section covering the authorised person's opinion of the assistance provided, can be submitted by authorised persons by filling in a questionnaire at the place where the assistance is provided, or submitted electronically directly to the office of the poviat district administration (Art. 7 (1a) of the LFLA).

Case documentation necessary for the provision of assistance may be kept at the centre for the duration of the assistance. Documentation submitted by the authorised person and documentation on the assistance provided may be attached to the assistance card after removing personal data from its content. In turn, it is the responsibility of the district governor to analyse the opinions of eligible persons about the assistance provided, taking into account the need to introduce improvements and increase the quality of free legal aid and free civic counselling (Art. 7 (4–5) of the Act). The statutory provisions are detailed in the Ordinance of the Minister of Justice of 15 December 2015 on the manner of providing and documenting free legal assistance.[73]

From the point of view of ensuring the organisation of this task, the Minister of Justice, who runs a central ICT system for the service of free legal aid, free civic counselling and legal education, is important. In particular, this ICT system processes data of persons:

1. reporting for an appointment;
2. providing free legal aid or free civic counselling; and
3. representing non-governmental organisations, district bar councils or district councils of chambers of legal advisers, employees of poviat district offices and provincial offices.

The administrators of the personal data processed in the system are The Minister of Justice, district governors and provincial governors, within the scope of the tasks covered by the Act. The data are processed for a period of five years from the end of the calendar year in which the tasks under the Act were completed,

---

72 See also: D. Daniluk, *Świadczenie nieodpłatnego poradnictwa obywatelskiego przez radcę prawnego lub adwokata a obowiązek zachowania tajemnicy zawodowej i unikania konfliktu interesów*, „Radca Prawny. Zeszyty Naukowe" 2022, nr 1(30), p. 33.

73 Dz. U. poz. 2492 z późn. zm.

with the exception of the personal data of applicants, which are processed for a period of one year from the end of the calendar year in which free legal advice or free civic counselling was provided (Art. 7a of the Act).

The district governor shall submit quarterly, through the competent Province Governor, to the Minister of Justice, aggregate information on the performance of the tasks of providing free legal assistance on the territory of the district by the end of the month following the end of the quarter (Art. 12 (1) of the LFLA). The conclusions from the analysis of the information for a given year, concerning the problems reported in the course of providing free legal aid and free civic counselling, indicating, in particular, current or projected needs in the field of free legal aid and free civic counselling, are posted on the website of the office serving the Minister of Justice by June 30 of the following year (Article 12 (5) of the LFLA).

3.5. Specific forms of providing free legal aid and free civic counselling

In particular, one should focus on the special forms of free legal aid and free civic counselling. In order to ensure the accessibility of free assistance services (including to persons with disabilities), the legislator offered beneficiaries so-called special forms under Article 8 (8) of the law under review. Essentially, persons with significant motor disabilities, unable to appear at the centre in person, and persons experiencing communication difficulties, as defined by the Act of 19 August 2011 on sign language and other means of communication,[74] may be provided with free legal aid (or free civic counselling), outside the centre (i.e. at the person's place of residence), or through means of remote communication (i.e. by telephone, email, instant messaging, video chat).

The organisation of the provision of free legal aid was noteworthy during the COVID-19 pandemic. Of fundamental importance for the functioning of the system of free legal aid and free civic counselling were the changes made by the Act of 14 May 2020 on amending some laws on protective measures in connection with the spread of the SARS-CoV-2 virus.[75] Article 28a was introduced into the Law on free legal aid, which provided the basis for the implementation of this task by means of distance communication. In light of this provision, in the event of an epidemic emergency, a state of epidemic or the introduction of

74 Dz. U. z 2017 r. poz. 1824.

75 Dz. U. poz. 875, z późn. zm.

a state of emergency, the provision of free legal aid or the provision of free civic counselling may be carried out by means of distance communication and off the centre's premises. As we have already emphasised, this solution was a response to social demand related to the existing epidemic threat and the need to guarantee health security. Thus, it is an instrument extending the possibility of providing legal advice outside the free legal aid centre.[76] The challenge facing Poland is to ensure a sufficient level of professionalism in the service provided (free legal aid/ free civic counselling).[77] There needs to be analysis into whether the functioning of various forms of assistance under free legal aid is fully justified, including in the context of rationalisation of public expenditure.

The extension of the circle of beneficiaries within the legal aid system to include entrepreneurs should also be viewed positively, which should be read as an attempt to minimise the negative socio-economic effects of the pandemic, in particular sole entrepreneurs. As part of protective solutions in connection with the spread of the SARS-CoV-2 virus, Article 4(1) of the LFLA was introduced, on the basis of which "free legal aid and free civic counselling shall be available to an eligible person who is unable to bear the costs of paid legal aid, including a natural person running a sole proprietorship that has not employed other persons in the past year". Prior to the amendment, free legal aid did not include "matters related to the conduct of economic activities, with the exception of preparation for the start of such activities". However, the question arises as to what criterion the legislator followed in excluding from the sphere of the assistance system entrepreneurs who employ other people. Such an entrepreneur may also find himself in a life situation requiring free legal assistance. In addition, the question arises about understanding the scope of the construction of "employment". This issue requires clarification.[78]

3.6. Funding of the free legal aid system

The task of providing free legal aid is financed from the state budget from the part at the disposal of the provincial governors by providing an earmarked subsidy to the poviats (Art. 19 (1) of the LFLA).[79] The financing of this task with

---

76 A. S. Bartnik, K. J. Kowalska, A. Krysztofowicz, *Nieodpłatna pomoc prawna online w czasach epidemii*, LEX/el. 2020.

77 See also: Wegner and Wróblewski, *Prawo*, p. 17.

78 It also draws attention to this: Daniluk, *Zmiany*, p. 141.

79 See also: WSA we Wrocławiu z 12 października 2017 r., IV SAB/Wr 115/17, LEX nr 2391598.

funds from the state budget is fully justified. This form of financing also occurs to some extent in other countries (see Table 1).

Table 1. Summary of basic information about the legal aid systems of selected countries with an indication of funding and governance

Country name	**Entities authorised**	**Scope of assistance available**	**Method of funding**	**Central management institution**
Germany	Persons in a difficult financial or personal situation.	The right to legal aid granted upon application processed by the local court. Assistance provided by a professional lawyer, reporting willingness to accept the case.	Funds provided in the budget of each state (Land).	No central governing body – legal aid system organised within each Land.
Sweden	Persons insured against legal aid costs incurred. State aid for the uninsured who meet the income criterion.	The terms and conditions of the legal assistance received vary depending on the insurance company. If you do not have adequate insurance, you should contact a local representative based in your area (an attorney or other qualified lawyer).	Legal aid insurance and state-funded assistance for those without such insurance.	Legal Aid Authority – reviews applications for legal aid.

Country name	Entities authorised	Scope of assistance available	Method of funding	Central management institution
France	Any person regardless of income – legal assistance in simple matters. Individuals without sufficient funds to finance legal advice.	Assistance provided by the so-called CDAD legal aid offices (Conseil departemental de l'accesses au droit) and houses of justice and law. The houses of justice and law provide advice on the simplest matters.	The state budget, the budget of the professional legal community and grants provided by local governments, public institutions and social security institutions.	CDAD (Conseil departemental de l'accesses au droit) – making decisions on the granting of legal aid and houses of justice and law (maisons de justices et du droit) – provide legal advice.
Netherlands	Persons meeting the income criterion, and in complicated cases, assistance provided on the basis of a certificate, specifying the amount of the fee necessary to be paid by the client.	Assistance provided by Legal Services Counters in uncomplicated cases, and in cases requiring extended assistance, by lawyers and mediators.	Assistance for low-income people is paid by the Legal Aid Board. The fee is based on the type of case and not the number of hours worked.	The Legal Aid Board is responsible for organising and administering the legal aid system. It also serves in an advisory capacity to the Ministry of Justice on matters relating to the public's need for and delivery of legal aid.

Country name	Entities authorised	Scope of assistance available	Method of funding	Central management institution
United Kingdom	Persons in financial distress whose legal problem qualifies for support. Legal aid services can only be provided by entities bound by contract with the Legal Aid Agency (LAA). These include certain attorneys, law offices and citizens' advice offices.	The legal aid system offers assistance differentiated according to the category of cases and the range of activities required, such as legal help (indications of rights and potential solutions), help at court, family mediation.	Assistance financed from the state budget, subject to the possibility of partial financing of the services provided, depending on the situation of the client and the outcome of the proceedings.	The Legal Services Commission (LSC) works with lawyers and NGOs.
Belgium	Persons meeting the income criterion, persons receiving social benefits, persons with disabilities, minors, foreigners, asylum seekers.	Legal information is provided at legal aid offices in each judicial district, public care centres and legal aid organisations. Detailed legal opinions or legal advice, including in the course of litigation, are pro-	Aid financed from the budget of the Ministry of Justice, and the activities of social organisations providing basic legal advice are financed from local budgets.	No central coordinating authority The Bureau for Legal Aid – coordination of legal aid at the stage of the court, at bar

Country name	**Entities authorised**	**Scope of assistance available**	**Method of funding**	**Central management institution**
		vided at legal aid offices established within the Bar by the Bar Council.		associations Legal Assistance Commissions – organise duty hours of lawyers and each operates according to its own rules.
Croatia	Persons who do not have sufficient funds to pay for legal advice and fall into one of the established categories (including foreigners who have been granted asylum in Croatia).	The granting of both pre-litigation and court legal aid requires the issuance of an administrative decision, and the recipient selects the lawyer himself. Lawyers, authorised associations, trade unions, as well as law faculties within the framework of law clinics operating within them are authorised to provide legal aid.	Aid financed from the state budget or local governments. Funds are provided to associations and law clinics on the basis of projects prepared by them. Co-financing of aid by its beneficiaries is allowed.	The system includes 20 State Office Administration regional offices that issue legal aid decisions.

Country name	**Entities authorised**	**Scope of assistance available**	**Method of funding**	**Central management institution**
Finland	Individuals without sufficient funds to finance legal advice.	A network of state legal aid offices where public legal aid attorneys provide assistance, as well as attorneys who are members of the Finnish Bar Association.	The aid is financed from the state budget in whole or in part, depending on the client's financial situation.	The Ministry responsible for Justice oversees the network of state legal offices.

Source: Information from the Supreme Audit Office, pp. 89–90.

The summary shows that in Germany, funding is provided in the budget of each land (Länder), while in France, funding comes from various sources:

(a) state budget;
(b) the budget of the professional self-government of lawyers; and
(c) grants provided by local governments, public institutions and social security institutions.

In the UK, legal aid is also funded from the state budget, but subject to the possibility of partial funding for the services provided depending on the client's situation and the outcome of the proceedings.

There is legal aid insurance in Sweden, but there is also, on the other hand, assistance in the form of partial funding or, in exceptional cases, full funding from the state budget for those without such insurance.

In Belgium, assistance is financed from the budget of the Ministry of Justice, and the activities of social organisations providing basic legal advice are financed from local budgets.

In Poland, the basic problem was the inefficiency of public funds allocated to finance the task of providing free legal aid. The audit of the Supreme Audit Office showed that there was a mismatch between the circle of beneficiaries of this assistance and the actual social needs and, on the other hand, the solution adopted of allowing funding only for the readiness to provide free legal assistance services.[80]

80 Informacja NIK, p. 13.

It is worth noting at this point that the Supreme Administrative Court[81] emphasised that in view of the norms of the Law on free legal assistance,

> including in particular those relating to the conditions and procedure of entrusting a non-governmental organisation with the conduct of points of free legal assistance, and then financing and accounting for this commissioned public task (...), it should be assumed that the information covered by the subject application of the Foundation of August 11, 2017 has the attribute of public information. The court of first instance correctly assumed that the contracts concluded by a non-governmental organisation with individuals for the implementation of free legal mediation as a public task, constitute public information. This is because there is no doubt that the information sought by the applicant relates to a public matter, i.e. contracts that were concluded with an entity performing public tasks financed from public funds.

This is important from the point of view of the realisation of the constitutional right of access to public information and, consequently, the transparency of the spending of public funds. From the jurisprudence of the administrative courts there is a broad concept of public information, which should be understood as "any news, concerning facts and data, produced by public authorities and persons performing public functions, as well as other entities that exercise this authority or manage municipal property or property of the State Treasury within the scope of their competence. News not produced by public entities, but relating to these entities, is qualified in the same way".[82]

Notwithstanding the comments raised, the creation – as complementary – of ways to maintain the system of free legal aid may be submitted for consideration. In particular, it is proposed to establish a Legal Aid Fund, which would be administered by the Council for Free Legal Aid and Legal Education. Funds from this fund would be used to improve the operation of the legal aid system. It was proposed that these funds would be provided from, among other things, donations and bequests.[83]

The introduction of relatively inexpensive but universal legal insurance[84] could also be considered. This solution could complement the legal aid system to some extent. However, it would require a broader analysis, especially in terms of

---

81 Wyrok NSA z 15 czerwca 2018 r., I OSK 1187/18, LEX nr 2509132.

82 Wyrok WSA we Wrocławiu z 25 maja 2018 r., IV SAB/Wr 27/18, LEX nr 2510555; see also cited case law: wyroki NSA z 30 października 2002 r., II SA 1956/02, LEX nr 78062 and 7 grudnia 2010 r., II OSK 1774/10, CBOSA.

83 Czernicki, *Dostęp*, pp. 926–927; Stanowisko przedstawicieli organizacji społecznych…, p. 6.

84 See also: Lipowicz, *O mądre*, p. 234.

determining possible state funding. We would also like to draw attention to the perceived – especially under the conditions in place during the COVID-19 pandemic – problems in connection with the use of services in the new technology market or the financial market. The generation of such problems may result in an increased need to protect consumers (clients) with the provision of free legal aid in particular.

3.7. Problem of quality of provision of free legal aid and free civic counselling

The law under review primarily provides reporting mechanisms on the implementation of the free legal aid service, and only control mechanisms to some extent.

Entrusting the provision of free legal advice to representatives of the public trust professions – attorneys and legal advisers – is fully justified, as it translates into the quality of the advice provided. Detailed rules for the exercise of legal professions of public trust have been regulated in individual so-called corporate laws. In the context of the quality of free legal advice provided by attorneys and legal advisers, the provisions of two laws are of particular importance:

1. Law of 26 May 1982 – Law on Advocacy (hereinafter: Law on Advocacy)[85]; and
2. Law of 6 July 1982 on legal advisors (hereinafter: Advisors Law).[86]

The basis for the guarantee of the appropriate quality of free legal advice can be sought in the regulations on the rules of practice of the profession of lawyer and legal adviser in terms of the quality of legal services provided. In this sphere, moreover, codes of ethics play an important role:

1. Collection of Principles of Bar Ethics and Dignity of the Profession (Code of Bar Ethics)[87]; and
2. Code of Ethics for Legal Advisors.[88]

In addition, it is necessary to point out the provisions of the aforementioned laws that relate directly to the issue of providing free legal advice. The tasks of the Bar

85 T.j. Dz. U. z 2022 r. poz. 1184 z późn. zm.

86 T.j. Dz. U. z 2022 r. poz. 1166.

87 See also: https://www.ora-warszawa.com.pl/wp-content/uploads/2018/04/Kodeks-Etyki-Adwokackiej.pdf (access: 22.12.2022).

88 See also: https://kirp.pl/etyka-i-wykonywanie-zawodu/etyka/kodeks-etyki-radcy-prawnego/ (access: 28.06.2022).

Association include: Cooperation with local self-government units for the implementation of the Act of 5 August 2015 on free legal aid (Article 3(1)(5a) of the Law on Advocates), and the scope of action of the Supreme Bar Council includes, in particular, the adoption of regulations on the rules for the appointment of attorneys to provide free legal aid (Article 58(12)(l) of the Law on Advocates).

Similarly, the Law on Legal Advisors (Article 41(5a) and Article 60 (8)(g)) provides for the same. The provision of erroneous information (legal assistance) may, in effect, result in the risk of liability for damages on the part of professional lawyers. It should be emphasised that a professional lawyer is subject to an annual obligation to pay a premium for liability insurance (Article 8a of the Law on Advocates and Article 22^7 of the Law on Advisors).[89]

Unlike those who provide legal advice professionally, those who do not have this status have not been required by the legislature to take out liability insurance for harming a client. The problem is that the legislator did not explicitly exclude their liability for providing incorrect advice. Only in Appendix No. 2 to the Law on Free Legal Aid, which is a model statement of a person benefiting from legal aid, is the following wording included: "I declare that I have been informed that any liability for damages of the person providing me with free legal aid is excluded, except in the case of damage caused by intentional fault."[90] From the point of view of the need to ensure the quality of the free legal advice provided, such a solution raises doubts.

Although the Law on Free Legal Aid does not indicate a legal definition of the term "quality of legal advice", nor does it provide for broad mechanisms to ensure the quality of the service, nonetheless some basic regulations in this regard can be identified. The difficulty lies primarily in the subjectivity of the assessments of the beneficiaries (people who use the service most often, who are not lawyers) as to the professionalism and reliability of the person providing the service. It remains necessary to define detailed indicators in law that would allow the quality and effectiveness of the system of free legal aid to be assessed. Proposals in this area were presented in the document prepared by the representatives of social organisations and titled Position of representatives of social organisations, members of the Council of Free Legal Aid and Legal Education to the Minister

89 See also: Judgment of the Supreme Administrative Court of April 27, 2021, II GSK 877/18, LEX No. 3184830; Judgment of the Supreme Administrative Court of April 18, 2019, II FSK 1275/17, LEX No. 2694771; Order of the Supreme Court of January 14, 2021, II DK 15/21, LEX No. 3106152.

90 Critically about this solution, see: Wegner and Wróblewski, *Prawo*, p. 13.

of Justice of 1 March 2017 on the summary of the year of operation and necessary changes in the Law on Free Legal Aid and Legal Education.[91] It emphasised the introduction of solutions to examine and evaluate the quality of legal aid provided. In particular, among the necessary changes postulated were: the organisation of appropriate training for service providers; the establishment of minimum standards for these services; the determination of the manner of documentation of the activities of those providing assistance; the introduction of the possibility of assessing client satisfaction (by completing anonymous questionnaires); cross-assessment by other lawyers (so-called *peer review*); and the development of indicators that would allow the quality and effectiveness of the system to be assessed.[92] The introduction into law of a mechanism for "accountability for failure to meet the quality of the assistance provided, resulting in removal from the list of service providers of free legal aid, or a periodic ban on entering into a contract for the provision of assistance in this system" was considered particularly important. These recommendations, in our view, remain valid and need to be implemented. The proposal to introduce basic guidelines for the quality of services provided and verification criteria at the statutory level on free legal aid should be submitted for consideration. It is particularly advisable to specify in the law solutions for liability for unreliable service provision (e.g. removal from the list of service providers).[93]

Further doubts are raised by the introduction of so-called free citizens' advice, consisting of activities tailored to the individual situation of the eligible party, aimed at raising awareness of his rights or obligations. As we have already indicated, the very idea of introducing free citizens' advice as an element of the state's activities – intended to raise the level of awareness (including legal awareness of the public) – is worth supporting. However, the problem remains at the level of practical application of the provisions on free civic counselling. The lack of a precise definition of this concept and verification criteria does not make it possible to conclude that there is an efficient system of free legal aid. Moreover, given the requirements for people to carry out this task (the so-called advisors),

91 Source https://bip.brpo.gov.pl/sites/default/files/Stanowisko%20cz%C5%82onk%C3%B3w%20Rady%20Nieodp%C5%82.%20Pom.%20Prawnej%20przy%20Ministrze%20Sprawiedliwo%C5%9Bci%2C%201.03.2017.pdf, p. 5 (access: 28.06.2022); also mentions these suggestions E. Gierach, *Kontrola jakości udzielanej nieodpłatnej pomocy prawnej* (text in the possession of the authors of the study).

92 E.g. Czernicki, *Dostęp*, p. 926.

93 E.g. Czernicki, *Dostęp*, p. 926.

this leads to a lowering of standards in citizens' legal security.[94] Let's note that legal advice falls within the area of free civic counselling, and it cannot be ruled out that in some cases – as practice shows – it will be the same as citizens' advice. The problem is that the counsellor is not obliged to keep confidential the information he learned while providing assistance, unless he is practicing as a lawyer (or legal counsellor). Again, the problem of documenting the public service provided remains.[95]

In the context of the issue addressed, the participation of NGOs should also be taken into account. They are obliged, among other things, to provide free civic counselling in a professional and reliable manner (Art. 11d par. 3 pt. 3(b) of the LFLA). In order to verify the aforementioned condition, the provincial governor evaluates selected advice provided in the provision of free civic counselling at the centre (Art. 11d para. 11 of the LFLA). Detailed regulations in this regard are contained in the Ordinance of the Minister of Justice on free legal aid and free civic counselling, according to which the provincial governor randomly selects at least 1% of the advice on free civic counselling provided at each centre located in the area of the poviats comprising the province.

The governor then submits the selected advice to an advisor with a recommendation from an entity authorised to organise training and retraining courses, instructing him to prepare a review of the submitted advice.[96]

It is worth at this point noting the problem of the quality-of-service provision by the NGO. For example, the Provincial Administrative Court[97] found the governor's assessment of the performance guarantee to be correct. This court emphasised the essence of the listing procedure – that is, assessing whether the non-governmental organisation applying for listing gives a guarantee of due performance of the public task, taking into account:

(a) its experience in this area;
(b) the existing way of performing the task; and
(c) its organisational and personnel capabilities.

94 Uchwała nr 79/2018 Prezydium Naczelnej Rady Adwokackiej z 19 czerwca 2018 r., p. 1; source http://www.adwokatura.pl/admin/wgrane_pliki/file-uchwala-nr-79-2018-23655.pdf (access: 28.06.2022).

95 It also pointed out in: Daniluk, *Świadczenie nieodpłatnego*, p. 37.

96 Daniluk, *Nieodpłatne poradnictwo*, pp. 48–49.

97 Wyrok WSA w Warszawie z 26.04.2022 r., VII SA/Wa 2433/21, LEX nr 3407140.

The court shared the Governor's arguments that the experience documented by the Foundation does not provide a guarantee of proper performance of the task, because despite having three years' experience in the implementation of tasks in the field of free legal aid, when entering competitions for the operation of points of free civic counselling in 2019, the Foundation showed a conscious and unreliable attitude towards the contracting authorities. In addition, this experience did not eliminate the irregularities associated with the referral of unqualified persons to provide free civic counselling in early 2019. The court found that the deficiencies in the Foundation's 2019 activities, due to their scale and nature, were serious enough to give the Governor grounds for assessing that the Foundation does not provide a guarantee of proper performance. However, in the Court's opinion, due to the discretionary nature of the decision to list the organisation, another authority in the same situation could find that the organisation's current human resources capabilities allow it to conclude that the Foundation meets the statutory prerequisites. The Foundation has obtained 2021 decisions to list organisations in several provinces. This circumstance will allow the Foundation, with the correct and professional fulfilment of its public task, to rebuild the authority's confidence in its reliability and credibility. For these reasons, the Court held that the appealed decision and the decision of the body of the first instance are in accordance with the law.

When addressing the issue of the quality provision of free legal aid and free civic counselling and the possibility of verifying the quality of the introduced system, attention should be paid to the catalogue of entities authorised to carry out this task. Attention should be paid to the closed circle of entities. In the first place, this service is carried out by professional attorneys (advocates and legal advisers), and exceptionally it can also be carried out – with the authorisation of an advocate or legal adviser – by trainee advocates and legal advisers and other persons trained in accordance with the law. Entrusting the provision of legal assistance to a trainee may be done only in particularly justified cases (Article 5(1) of the LFLA). This would take into account fortuitous situations and difficult-to-surmount obstacles to the personal provision of this public service. Referring to the formula of the exceptional nature of the representation of an advocate (respectively, a legal counsel) by trainees, it should be noted that on the basis of the current legislation there is no justification for imposing on them the obligation to provide legal assistance in full. It is worth noting that on the basis of Article 77(3) of the law on advocacy, it is permissible for a trainee legal adviser to substitute an advocate – on the same terms as a legal adviser – "if the advocate is a partner in an advocate-counsel partnership, except for cases in which the advocate acts as a defence counsel in criminal proceedings and in proceedings for fiscal offences".[98] Hence, it seems that the regulation of Article 5(1) of the LFLA does not violate the aforementioned rules. At the same time, the basis for the provision of free legal aid (free civic counselling) in this case is Article 6(1) of the LFLA, providing for a contract concluded between an advocate (legal counsellor) and the poviat.[99]

Thus, the scope of the lawyer's (legal counsel's) duties under the contract is of primary importance. For example, Article 5(3) of the LFLA provides a basis for waiving this obligation only for important reasons but must inform the entitled person about other centres offering free legal assistance in the poviat. Such a case of refusal to provide service may be circumstances arising from the so-called conflict of interest. It is also impossible to exclude cases in which legal advice would cover very specialised areas of law. This understanding is supported by Article 8, paragraph 9, sentence 1, of the LFLA, from which it follows that all or certain of the duty hours of a lawyer at a centre may have a specific specialisation. Thus, it indicates that it is possible to distinguish the fields of law or issues of free legal assistance provided (respectively, free civic counselling).[100]

Further doubts arise against the background of Article 11(3) of the LFLA, which provides for the possibility of providing free legal aid at centres entrusted to a non-governmental organisation by:

1) a tax advisor – in the field of tax law, excluding business tax matters;
2) a person who:
   a) graduated from higher legal studies and obtained a master's degree or foreign legal studies recognised in the Republic of Poland,
   b) has at least three years' experience in performing activities requiring legal knowledge directly related to the provision of legal assistance,
   c) enjoys full public rights and has full legal capacity,
   d) has not been convicted of an intentional crime prosecuted by public indictment or a fiscal crime [...].

Analysis of these norms of the Law on Free Legal Aid raises several observations in the context of the quality-of-service provision and the possibility of verifying the free legal aid system. Persons providing legal assistance who do not have the status of a professional – unlike entities professionally engaged in providing

98 More on that: J. Trela, [in:] *Prawo o adwokaturze. Komentarz*, red. P. Kruszyński, Warszawa 2016, LEX, komentarz do art. 77 pr. adw.
99 See: Wegner and Wróblewski, *Prawo*, p. 11.
100 Wegner and Wróblewski, *Prawo*, pp. 11–12.

legal advice (attorneys, legal advisers) – have not been obliged by the legislator to conclude a civil liability insurance contract for causing damage to the client. Hence, the question arises as to the level of preparation of the persons whom the NGO has selected? In particular, there is a problem in verifying the preparation of these persons, since the legislator allowed this group of people to provide the service of free legal aid, or free civic counselling. From Appendix No. 2 to the Law on Free Legal Aid (which is a model statement of a person benefiting from legal aid), the following wording is included:

> I declare that I have been informed that any liability for compensation of the person providing me with free legal assistance is excluded, except in the case of damage caused by intentional fault. I acknowledge that the person providing me with free legal assistance is not obliged to maintain secrecy, within the meaning of Article 180 § 2 of the Act of June 6, 1997. – Code of Criminal Procedure.[101]

In light of this provision:

> Persons obliged to maintain notarial, attorney, legal counsel, tax advisor, medical, journalistic or statistical secrecy, as well as the secrecy of the Public Prosecutor General's Office, may be questioned as to the facts covered by this secrecy only if it is necessary for the interests of justice and the circumstance cannot be established by other evidence. In pre-trial proceedings, the questioning or permission for questioning shall be decided by the court, in a session without the participation of the parties, within no more than 7 days from the date of service of the prosecutor's request.

In addition, the appendix states:

> I declare that I have been informed that submission of the above statement is voluntary. I (have) familiarised myself with the contents of the above statement and agree to receive free legal assistance in accordance with the above conditions.

In our view, the solution adopted raises many doubts. The provider of legal advice (who is not an advocate or legal adviser) is not obliged to instruct the individual about the rules and consequences of using this service. One should notice the inconsistency of the legislator. It follows from Article 11(4) of the LFLA that in the case referred to in paragraph 3(2) of the LFLA (concerning a person who: (a) graduated from a higher legal education institution and obtained a master's degree or foreign legal studies recognised in the Republic of Poland; (b) has at least three years' experience in performing activities that require legal

---

101 Tekst jedn. Dz.U. z 2022 r. poz. 1375; see also: M. Kurowski, [in:] *Kodeks postępowania karnego*, t. 1, *Komentarz aktualizowany*, red. D. Świecki, LEX 2021, komentarz do art. 180.

knowledge and are directly related to the provision of legal assistance; (c) enjoys full public rights and has full legal capacity; and (d) has not been convicted of an intentional crime prosecuted by public indictment or a fiscal crime) an eligible person, before obtaining free legal assistance, shall submit a written statement that he is aware of obtaining free legal assistance from a person who is not an advocate, legal adviser or tax adviser). However, in the appendix to the Law there is a model of this statement providing for a number of clauses, including referring to the aforementioned limitation of civil liability. Even more questionable is the content of the model statement, that is, the instruction that the legal aid provider is not obliged to maintain defence secrecy.[102]

A way of verifying the quality of the services provided, and thus planning the organisation of the assistance provided, is the opinions of eligible beneficiaries, in which a questionnaire, that is, Part B assistance card, is used to collect information. This method involves obtaining data by analysing the answers to survey questions of a closed-ended nature and an open-ended question aimed at comments and possible proposals for improving activities. The important thing is that the surveys are voluntary, anonymous, and the results are not linked to a specific person.[103]

According to the 2021 report of the Minister of Justice, some beneficiaries of the free assistance system – 89.72% – "were very satisfied with the assistance they received". The highest ratings (97.24%) were received for the question "Were you received at the centre on the agreed date?", while the lowest results (78.38%) were obtained for the question "Is the premises where the centre is located clearly marked?" In addition, the group of beneficiaries satisfied with the assistance received includes those who marked the answer "rather yes", which increases the pool of positive answers by another 9.42%.[104]

We draw attention to the practice of applying the norms of the Law on Free Legal Aid. This was reflected, in particular, in the judgment of the PAC in Warsaw of 11 May 2021, VII SA/Wa 345/21[105]; the Court, after recognising at a closed session on 11 May 2021 the case from the complaint of the H. Foundation against the decision of the Minister of Justice on the entry on the list of non-governmental organisations authorised to conduct points for the provision

102 The above-mentioned doubts are highlighted by: Wegner and Wróblewski, *Prawo*, pp. 12–13.
103 Ocena sprawozdania Ministra Sprawiedliwości za 2021 r., p. 43.
104 Ocena sprawozdania Ministra Sprawiedliwości za 2021 r., p. 45.
105 LEX nr 3265710.

of free civic counselling, dismissed the complaint. On the basis of the evidence gathered in the case, the Court found that, in addition to the Foundation's withdrawal from the concluded agreements, there were a number of other irregularities in the course of their execution in several other poviats.

The problem boiled down to the fact that the Foundation was directing lawyers who were not yet qualified to provide civic counselling to the on-call centres. In addition, the Court found that the Foundation did not report absences from on-call services; it was unable to ensure stable staffing of the on-call free civic counselling centres, due to the failure to allow Foundation associates to take the exam for civic counsellors. As a result, according to the Court, such action "resulted in the partial duty of legal advisors and attorneys without a certificate of completion of the civic advisor course", and the Foundation "did not carry out its duty at the centres according to the schedule of the centre's operation in the Municipality [...] which consisted in the failure to carry out in the months of January and February 2019 48 on-call hours in the Municipality of [...] and 66 on-call hours in the Municipality of [...]". With this in mind, in the Court's view:

> The Minister of Justice therefore reasonably assumed that the Foundation's actions and omissions were not incidental, the occurrence of which was accidental and beyond the Foundation's control. Indeed, the reasons for not signing the agreement or withdrawing from it were the lack of appropriately qualified personnel capable of providing citizen counselling.

The Court shared the argumentation of the Minister of Justice that in the analysed case

> the situations were not caused by reasons on the part of the poviats, but resulted from the applicant's unsupported-by-the-facts assessment of its own staff capabilities, formulated despite the lack of a sufficient number of qualified persons meeting the statutory requirements who could perform civic counselling activities. The Foundation, without a proper assessment of its ability to properly perform the tasks of providing free civic counselling, entered numerous competitions. This was a conscious and dependent action on the part of the Foundation.

Thus:

> The Court shares the position of the Minister of Justice that, based on the situations described in the decision, it is reasonable to conclude that the Foundation did not provide a guarantee of due performance in the task of providing free civic counselling. The Foundation's actions of entering competitions despite the lack of suitable persons who could perform civic counselling, as well as the cases of directing such persons to perform the task, testify to the misleading of the relevant district governors and the conscious application for this task despite the lack of capacity to perform it. This resulted in disruptions in the organisation of free legal aid and free civic counselling at the respective

district governors, including the need to turn to other entities in an appropriate manner to provide service to these centres, as a result of which no free civic counselling was provided at the centres until that time.

We believe that it would be more appropriate to use qualified individuals in the legal profession with relevant knowledge and experience. For example, one could include trainee attorneys and counsellors who already have some legal knowledge and experience. This is a solution that is present in the Swedish system, where a lawyer's assistant is also authorised to give advice. There is a real concern that, in practice, the performance of this public task will be carried out at different levels of professionalism, and will consequently raise legitimate questions from the point of view of preserving the principle of equality.

Currently, those providing free legal assistance have an obligation of a reporting nature as to the subject and object scope of the provision of this service. In the opinion of the authors, despite the passage of several years, the current legislation does not provide a basis for full verification of the quality of services provided. This is especially true for those who are selected by NGOs. In turn, the maintenance of this state of affairs does not serve the realisation of reliability and efficiency in public institutions, and it is the state's responsibility to construct the system of free legal aid in the country in such a way that each beneficiary can receive it at uniformly high level of professionalism.[106]

3.8. Task implementation practice

A report by the Supreme Audit Office shows that in 2016 and 2017 (up to and including November) a total of 180,343 thousand zlotys (93,193 thousand zlotys and 87,150 thousand zlotys, respectively)[107] were transferred to poviats from the state budget for the implementation of this task in the form of an earmarked grant. For the indicated purpose, the audited units spent a total of PLN 3,861.3 thousand in 2016 (99% of the sum of the planned amounts). In the first half of 2017. PLN 1,760.6 thousand (45% of the planned amounts). These funds were mainly allocated for payment of salaries for the provision of assistance by attorneys (legal advisors), payment of targeted subsidies from the budget of local government units granted to finance or subsidise tasks commissioned to non-governmental organisations. They were also allocated for the purchase of materials and equipment for free assistance centres. These expenses were incurred in

106 Przywora, *Normatywny*, p. 403.
107 Informacja NIK, p. 14.

observance of the principle specified in the Law on free legal assistance, namely allocating 97% of the subsidy to remuneration for contracts with attorneys and legal advisers and to the non-governmental organisation selected in the open tender, and 3% of the subsidy to cover the costs of organisational and technical support for this task.[108]

The Supreme Audit Office pointed to broadcasts from the Ministry of Justice, which show that in 2016, nationwide, the average cost of one piece of advice (calculated as the ratio of the sum of the entity's expenses) incurred in carrying out the task to the number of pieces of advice provided during the period (drawn up by lawyers of the free legal aid cards) amounted to PLN 202.74 (gross amount). At the centres run by attorneys or legal advisers – PLN 184.67 gross, and at the centres entrusted to NGOs – PLN 234.21 gross. On the territory of the poviats covered by the audit in 2016 and the first half of 2017, the cost ranged from PLN 101.61 to PLN 3,373.66, while the average was PLN 341.04 and PLN 333.81 (for centres run by attorneys or legal advisers) and PLN 471.97 and PLN 602.15 (for centres run by NGOs), respectively. Consequently, the SAO's analysis shows that the unit cost of advice ranged from PLN 101.61 to PLN 3,373.66, and the significant spread of these values was due to the difference in the number of pieces of advice provided at the various centres run in the area of the controlled units.[109]

Against this background, it is important to note the 2020 data. In the first quarter of 2020, 110,667 instances of free legal aid and free civic counselling were provided, while in the second quarter there were only 45,186. Although the numbers in the third (89,685) and fourth (69,853) quarters increased, they did not reach a level similar to the first quarter. An analysis of the data shows a decrease of about 28% in the quantity of advice compared to the previous year, when a total of 455,055 was provided. In 2020, there were 743 centres run by attorneys and legal counsellors and 779 centres run by NGOs.[110] In 2020, the majority of assistance went to beneficiaries with low net income per person in the household – 65.96% of beneficiaries had a monthly income in the range of PLN 600–2000. On the other hand, the smallest share of aid went to those who declared no income (6.79%), and in second place to those whose income per person in the household was below PLN 600 (10.2%). A relatively large share of assistance (17.1%) went to beneficiaries who declared an income higher than PLN 2,000.[111]

---

108 Informacja NIK, p. 14.

109 Informacja NIK, p. 14.

110 Ocena Ministra Sprawiedliwości za 2020 r., p. 37.

111 Ocena Ministra Sprawiedliwości za 2020 r., p. 37.

On a positive note, the possibility of providing advice outside the centre or by means of remote communication, due to the pandemic, has also been extended to all beneficiaries, not just those with disabilities. Due to the protection of personal data and sensitive information, if advice is provided in this manner, the obligation for the beneficiary to provide a declaration of inability to bear the cost of the service or, in the case of entrepreneurs, of not employing others in the past year has been removed.[112]

Against this background, it is reasonable to point to the data resulting from the Minister of Justice's report for 2021.[113] Both for the category of free legal aid and for the category of free civic counselling, it was found that the most frequently used special form of assistance was the telephone form included in the remote advice. This form was used in 171,526 cases, accounting for 95.61% of the total special forms. The percentage of beneficiaries using other forms of assistance provided remotely, which include instant messaging such as email, instant messaging, video chat, accounted for only 6,729 cases, or 3.75%.[114]

According to the Ministry of Justice, there has been an adaptation to pandemic realities in 2021. There has been an increase in the provision of free legal aid and free civil counselling:

(a) in 2020, 315,391 pieces of advice were provided; and
(b) in 2021, they provided 388,891 pieces of advice.

From this comes an increase of 0.23%.

There is also a change in the percentage distribution between free legal aid and free civic counselling. The implementation of free civic counselling from 2019 translates into a successive increase in the amount of advice provided in this regard:

(a) in 2019, free civic counselling accounted for 11.84% of the counselling provided;
(b) in 2020 – 16.23%; and
(c) in 2021 – 19.61%.

112 Ocena Ministra Sprawiedliwości za 2020 r., p. 39.
113 Ocena Ministra Sprawiedliwości z realizacji zadań z zakresu nieodpłatnej pomocy prawnej, nieodpłatnego poradnictwa obywatelskiego oraz edukacji prawnej za 2021 rok.
114 Ocena Sprawiedliwości za 2021 r., p. 42.

The results of the continued 2021 non-standard channels for the provision of services foreseen in the event of an epidemic emergency, a state of epidemic or the introduction of a state of emergency, that is, by means of remote communication, indicate that the search for innovations in this regard can contribute to increasing the effectiveness of legal aid. In 2021, in 171,526 cases, assistance was provided by telephone. On this basis, a conclusion can be drawn about the legitimacy of supporting standard forms of assistance provision (the so-called stationary mode) by a non-standard one (the so-called remote mode), and facilitating access to the latter without having to meet the prerequisites of Article 28a of the Law can be very beneficial to beneficiaries of legal aid.[115] The study shows that willingness to seek legal aid is most strongly dependent on the type of problem. The largest amount of advice was given in civil and family law. The problems of beneficiaries were mainly related to: statutory inheritance, claiming alimony, termination of marriage, children, disposition of property, loans and credits, acquisition and regulation of property, aggrievement, court proceedings and claims for damage caused.

The main source of knowledge about the legal aid system is the Internet (35.39%) and other clients of the centres (34.31%). The survey proves the untapped capital of the media (press, radio, television) in promoting the free assistance system. According to the satisfaction surveys (Card B), knowledge of the legal aid system from the aforementioned media accounts for only 4.02% of all sources of information. Underlying this thesis, that is, the social impact of the mass media, is the knowledge of the information potential of the press, radio and television. The effect of media exclusion is the continuing low public awareness of the legal aid system. It can be said that the services of the free assistance system are most often used by people:

(a) aged 35–55 years old (38.47%);
(b) with secondary vocational and basic vocational education (51.40%); and
(c) earning income above 1,000–1,500 and above 2,000 (45.79%), the source of which is work (40.28%).[116]

The free legal aid and free civic counselling system include the possibility to control its effectiveness by having beneficiaries fill out an assistance card B, which allows them to express their opinion about the advice given. Analysis of statistical data allows us to conclude that beneficiaries are significantly satisfied with

115 Ocena Ministra Sprawiedliwości za 2021 r., p. 48.
116 Ocena Ministra Sprawiedliwości za 2021 r., p. 50.

the assistance they received. Customers highly rated both the friendly welcome, the comprehensible presentation of information, the convenience of the location and the legibility of the centre's signage, as well as the timeliness of the advice and the elaboration on the next steps to be taken. The possibility of obtaining advice by means of remote communication was also positively received – the desire to retain this means was demonstrated even after the pandemic.[117]

In the beneficiaries' evaluation of the system's performance, there were instances of dissatisfaction with issues concerning the legibility of the premises' signage, the convenience of the centre's location and awareness of what steps to take next. This fact highlights the need to improve these aspects of service. Restrictions on movement caused by the imposition of restrictions meant that the evaluation of the accessibility of the centres was not entirely satisfactory. The solution should be greater use of the possibility of creating mobile centres.[118]

Against this background, the proposals of the Ministry of Justice are worth focusing on. In particular, the proposal to completely abolish the obligation to submit a written statement on the inability to bear the cost of paid legal aid is worth noting – it often constitutes a psychological barrier for those seeking assistance that is difficult to overcome. Also under consideration is the introduction, not only during epidemic periods, of remote provision of assistance as a permanent option, the choice of which would be up to the beneficiary of the assistance. This solution has proven itself in difficult times and its continuation is expected by society. It will allow the abolition of regionalisation, reducing the burden on the most beleaguered centres, and adding to the workload of the least effective ones.[119]

The practice of organising periodic meetings with poviats is being introduced to enable effective communication and a steady flow of information to quickly introduce new facilities in the system of free legal aid and free civic counselling. In addition, it is planned to organise training for contractors in the field of free civic counselling and in the ICT system for handling free assistance.[120]

117 Ocena Ministra Sprawiedliwości za 2020 r., p. 39.

118 Ocena Ministra Sprawiedliwości za 2020 r., p. 39.

119 Ocena Ministra Sprawiedliwości za 2020 r., pp. 40–41.

120 Ocena Ministra Sprawiedliwości za 2020 r., p. 41.

Conclusions

Poland has had a formalised system of free legal aid for several years. Its 2018 reform led to significant changes that included, in particular, beneficiaries of legal aid. The catalogue of entities was expanded by replacing the positive enumeration formula with a general clause. Such a solution simplified to some extent the mechanism for verifying the beneficiaries of this public service. Analysing the statistical data contained in the 2022 report of the Minister of Justice on the implementation of free legal aid, it should be said that to some extent they have contributed to improving the efficiency of the system, increasing the availability of this public service (especially by individuals). As a result, it can be said that it is more fully possible to realise the right to a court and other rights, so the modified solutions more fully rationalise the process of legal measures. It is also more widely possible to provide this service especially when operating in the COVID-19 pandemic state.

However, it remains a challenge to strengthen the level of professionalism in the service provided (free legal aid/free civic counselling).[1] Hence, the current norms should be regarded as a step towards building an optimal system. However, in many cases, the solutions adopted in 2018 raise doubts, including of a constitutional nature. It seems reasonable to undertake a debate on the shape of further changes in the area of free legal assistance at the pre-litigation stage (free civic counselling, legal education and the institution of mediation require changes), especially with regard to the scope of the subject matter, as well as the principles of its organisation. In particular, an unambiguous determination is required to define the relationship between free legal aid and free civic counselling. Taking into account the specificity of Polish conditions, we find the Ukrainian and Swedish norms discussed in the paper inspiring.

In further discussions, the following directions should be taken into account. We propose formally separating information from legal advice requiring a commitment to prepare the first pleading in a case, and to define legal information as generally available. In this case, it would require the gradation of the free legal aid service into basic and qualified. Taking the remote mode of providing basic legal assistance (information) into account, it should be recognised that its beneficiaries could be all interested citizens, or even all persons residing in

1 See also: Wegner and Wróblewski, *Prawo*, p. 17.

the territory of the Republic of Poland. This assistance, however, would be limited only to providing information on the current legal status and the rights and obligations arising therefrom. Such a solution would be more useful from an economic perspective of the law, for with the same organisational costs it will allow greater access to the right to a court and the principle of social justice. All the more so, since the process of providing free legal aid at this level can involve, for example, trainee attorneys and counsellors to a greater extent. According to the National Council of the Judiciary:

> the involvement of qualified lawyers should be evaluated positively, however, limiting ourselves only to advocates and legal advisers is the most expensive and inefficient solution. This is because the solutions operating in the world focus on organising the system in such a way that the cases that require it go to the attorneys, and others are solved by qualified counsel.[2]

The idea is that a structured system of free legal aid at the pre-litigation stage should be (as a last resort) a bridge to the effective assertion of rights already at the court stage.

As the most objective – following (for example) the Swedish solutions – the income criterion should be adopted. Consistently, we take the position that making the right to legal aid dependent on earned income in relation to the amount of the minimum wage is an objective criterion that constitutes the basis for granting an additional benefit from the state.

The second type of legal aid is the so-called qualified legal aid, addressed to strictly defined persons in a difficult life situation and with a low material status, verified by means of an income criterion. This solution would be in line with the realisation of the principles, rights and protective duties discussed in the work, consisting in public authorities taking action to protect the weaker individual. For example, such a group of beneficiaries could include an entrepreneur who found himself in a difficult financial situation due to the constraints of the COVID-19 pandemic. As a positive direction of change, we assess the expansion of the circle of beneficiaries within the legal aid system to include entrepreneurs, in particular sole proprietors, as a reduction in the negative socio-economic effects of the pandemic. As part of the shielding solutions for the spread of the SARS-CoV-2 virus, Article 4(1) of the LFLA was introduced, on the basis of which "free legal aid and free civic counselling shall be available to an eligible

---

2 Opinia Krajowej Rady Sądownictwa z 16.01.2015 r. w przedmiocie projektu ustawy o nieodpłatnej pomocy prawnej i informacji prawnej, pp. 1–2, source: https://www.adwokatura.pl/admin/wgrane_pliki/file-opiniakrspomoc-10974.pdf (access: 02.07.2022).

person who is unable to bear the costs of paid legal aid, including a natural person running a sole proprietorship that has not employed other persons in the past year". However, under further amendments, entrepreneurs who employ other people should be included in the assistance system. Such an entrepreneur may find himself in a life situation requiring free legal assistance. It is also reasonable to clarify the concept of "employment".[3]

Thirdly, doubts are raised by the introduction of the so-called free civic counselling, which includes activities tailored to the individual situation of the entitled person, aimed at raising awareness of their rights or obligations. In our opinion, the functioning of this solution in free legal aid implies a number of doubts, including those of compatibility with the Constitution of the Republic of Poland. The legislator should not use the indefinite concept of "civic counselling", as this causes many problems of interpretation. In particular, the legislator does not specify what relation this concept has to the already functioning institution of free legal aid. The lack of a precise definition of this concept will lead to lower standards of legal security of citizens in the process of implementation of this task.[4] There is also no justification for introducing a new category of persons to handle this task – the so-called counsellors. The requirements for advisors significantly deviate from the standards that give a guarantee of reliable performance of civic counselling, expected of a person providing legal advice. With the above in mind, it is our position that the system of free legal aid should be as informal and easy to "operate" as possible, both for those using it (beneficiaries) and those providing it. There should be no doubt as to whether an activity still falls within the scope of a given public service or not? Hence the need to simplify the system of free legal aid. What remains to be considered is the remodelling of free civic counselling in such a way that the division between legal aid and civic counselling is clear and feasible in practice. Efforts should be made to use the potential of both professional attorneys (advocates, legal advisers), as well as trainee attorneys and trainee legal advisers. However, the introduction of additional persons into the system (e.g. counsellors) should be abandoned. This is because the point is to guarantee free legal assistance at the highest possible level of professionalism, and this requires not only legal expertise but also many years of experience.[5]

---

3 It also draws attention to this: Daniluk, *Zmiany*, p. 141.

4 Uchwała nr 79/2018 Prezydium Naczelnej Rady Adwokackiej z 19 czerwca 2018 r., p. 1.

5 See also: Daniluk, *Free counselling*, p. 53–54.

In particular, we draw attention to the problem of verifying the quality of free legal aid services (free civic counselling). We see the need to specify (e.g. by poviat units) uniform and precise criteria to be met by NGOs applying for free legal aid. The point is to ensure proper standards for the performance of legal services.

The comments made are crucial from a constitutional perspective and from the perspective of improving the free legal aid system. Notwithstanding the findings made, it is still worth noting a few important points.

We also draw attention to the problem of financing this task. Its implementation (preferably at the local level) and state funding are justified. This is supported by the special nature of this task anchored in the right to social assistance and the constitutional guarantee of the right to a court. On the other hand, the creation of complementary ways to maintain the system can be submitted for consideration. As an example, it has been proposed to establish a Legal Aid Fund, the dispositor of which would be the Council for Free Legal Aid and Legal Education,[6] or to introduce a relatively inexpensive but universal legal insurance.[7] These solutions could complement the legal aid system to some extent.

Attention should also be paid to the need to define the relationship between the various institutions providing free pre-litigation legal assistance. In particular, it is necessary to point out the different regulations stipulating the formula for providing counselling.

The authors of the report are convinced that the system of free legal aid (free civic counselling or legal education) should to some extent make use of the achievements of ombudsman-like institutions, with particular emphasis on the Ombudsman for Civil Rights and the Ombudsman for Children. The role of the Ombudsman is to protect the freedoms and rights of citizen and mankind set forth in the Constitution of the Republic of Poland and other normative acts (Article 208(1) of the Constitution of the Republic of Poland), while the Ombudsman for Children will guard the observance of children's rights (Article 72(1) and (4) of the Constitution of the Republic of Poland). Implementation of the tasks incumbent on them primarily boils down to providing expert legal information (advice) to applicants about their rights. In this regard, it is necessary to determine the interrelationship between their responsibilities and the entities performing the task under the Law on Free Legal Aid.

---

6 Stanowisko przedstawicieli organizacji społecznych…, p. 6.

7 See: Lipowicz, *O mądre*, p. 234.

It is also worth considering structuring the system for providing free legal aid in a single legal act. To some extent, this would improve the efficiency of carrying out this task at both pre-litigation and court levels, and thus would be part of realising the right to good administration, which is an important part of the *right to good governance* in a democratic state under the rule of law.[8] Hence, the steps already taken to improve the system of free legal aid through the use of electronic tools should be appreciated. This is particularly beneficial under the conditions operating during the COVID-19 pandemic. Making this service available largely remotely could increase its attractiveness.

At the end of the conclusions section, it is reasonable to summarise the comparative legal analysis. The juxtaposition of solutions adopted in the Ukrainian legal system and in the Kingdom of Sweden presents a picture of two different systems that offer solutions for ensuring the quality of legal aid in the broader sense.

Ukrainian solutions, although relatively new, provide for multi-faceted control of the quality of advice provided in primary legal aid. At the same time, the carrier of information about the quality of the legal aid provided in the broad sense is no longer the client to whom the advice is given, but the specialists who carry out random checks in the form of "peer review". At the same time, this is a system that has the makings of being effective, but its biggest drawback is certainly its costliness. This is due to the fact that it provides for a central legal aid authority, within it a quality control authority for free legal aid, as well as regional quality managers.

In contrast, when analysing Swedish solutions, it should be emphasised that they are the product of years of experience. Consequently, it is a system of transferring the provision of legal aid and legal advice to law firms and hence partial privatisation. Thus, this solution implies that the Swedish Bar Council is responsible for quality control. At the same time, this solution is not completely detached from state control. It should be noted that the advocacy profession in the Swedish system is regulated differently from Polish solutions. Central to the advocacy profession are the provisions of the aforementioned Code of Judicial Procedure.[9] Such a solution means that many powers in relation to the lawyer are also held by the court, which leads to a situation of double control

8 Compare: H. Izdebski, *Zasada dobrej administracji i prawo do dobrej administracji w świetle standardów Rady Europy*, [in:] *60 lat Rady Europy. Tworzenie i stosowanie standardów prawnych*, red. H. Machińska, Warszawa 2009, p. 323 i n.

9 This is an act regulating the professions of advocate, prosecutor and judge. It contains regulations on common courts and provisions on civil and criminal proceedings.

over the quality of the lawyer's performance. On the one hand, it is the Swedish Bar Council, and on the other, it is the court at any time within the framework of court proceedings or as the final instance in the case of supervision of attorneys' activities.

Despite the differences, Ukrainian and Swedish solutions have common elements, namely corporate control within the framework of free legal aid. From the point of view of the construction of the Polish system of civic counselling, Ukrainian solutions may seem closer. This is due to the fact that there is a similar structure of civic counselling. The Ukrainian experience indicates the need to shift the burden of quality control in the Polish system from clients to specialists who supervise the implementation of tasks within the framework of civic counselling. This will allow a real picture of legal aid to be presented and, moreover, will contribute to filling the gaps in the system by creating training courses or establishing a tutoring system. Swedish solutions, on the other hand, provide a basis for greater involvement in the process of quality control of both citizen counselling and legal aid by legal corporations.

The process of assessing (verifying) the quality of the service provided is subjective, and therefore subject to the risk of lack of due diligence and reliability. This is largely due to the fact that people who use legal assistance are usually not lawyers and are not, in most cases, able to reliably assess the merits of legal assistance (advice). On the other hand, they can assess the approach of the person providing legal assistance (advice), as well as the form of the message as to how to solve the problem. This is all the more difficult because it is often only in the course of several meetings that it is possible to present the totality of the materials in the case necessary for the preparation of a pleading and skilfully present the problem. Under such conditions, a person without adequate professional training and experience will not be able to fully read the intentions of the beneficiary of the service. This is because in many cases effectiveness depends on immediate action.

Another problem relates to the reliability of customer surveys (beneficiaries of the free legal aid service). It is not a problem that they are – in principle – positive, but the lack of gradation of this evaluation makes it relatively unreliable in terms of making improvement changes. Therefore, it is increasingly proposed, as one of the solutions, that the quality of the provision of free legal aid should be evaluated by people with expertise within the framework of "peer review" inspections. There should also be other verification solutions in the system to "capture" problems and create solutions to provide a viable response.

We recommend the wider use of the online method of communication in the provision of free legal aid service, especially in situations that do not require personal direct contact. This type of solution – as shown in practice during the conditions of the COVID-19 pandemic – promotes the use of the free legal aid (advice) service. Important in this regard is the system of notification (registration) to the free legal aid centre.

In the process of improving the operation of the system of free legal aid, the proposals contained in the report of the Minister of Justice, in particular, may be important:

1. taking into account the specifics of the free legal aid service and adapting it to social needs in particular (e.g. through the creation of specialised duty stations);
2. to a greater extent, intervening at an early stage in relation to the problems experienced, including through legal education of the public;
3. introducing innovative ways of providing services so that they are most responsive to the needs of the beneficiary group and receive its recognition;
4. implementation of a single (unified) set of standards that all service providers should be required to follow;
5. bridging the barriers of access to free legal aid and free civic counselling (easily accessible, clear signage of the centres, providing differentiated access channels – remote or in situ depending on the choice of the eligible person), and above all by carrying out skilful and effective information and promotional activities (this also applies to undertaking educational activities and creating an appropriate organisational culture; e.g. appropriate definition of needs at the stage of enrolment for advice); and
6. ensuring adequate reporting to collect data on the legal problems of eligible persons, evaluating data on beneficiaries, assessing their satisfaction.[10]

10 Ocena Ministra Sprawiedliwości za 2021 r., pp. 50–52.

Proposed models

One of the objectives of this work was to compare the solutions adopted in the legal systems studied. As already mentioned, the choice of countries for comparative legal research was not accidental. On the one hand, the authors chose the United Kingdom, where the system of citizens' advice dates back to the Second World War. It is a remarkably interesting system based solely on funding legal advice organisations in the form of grants from the state. However, it is a system in which there is a noticeable blurring of the boundaries between counselling and legal aid. For example, the subjective judgment of an employee providing legal advice to refer a person using the benefit to an on-call lawyer. This should be considered a more than desirable solution, as it demonstrates the effectiveness in this financial solution adopted in the UK,[1] which is often considered a budget "sink" without demonstrating the benefits it brings to the system. At the same time, we are talking about benefits not only in the form of supporting the realisation of citizens' rights and freedoms, but also those in the form of savings for the budget.

From the point of view of the Polish system, the financing of the provision of legal aid in the form of grants is difficult to accept. The method of financing itself is not an advantage due to the lack of certainty of continuity of assistance provided within the framework of civic counselling – not only for organisations providing such advice, but also for citizens themselves. On the other hand, the system is geared to provide for as many "clients" as possible and thus the scope of citizens' advice provided in the UK is very wide. In the UK, it is necessary – due to the grant-based system – to demonstrate the legitimacy of the system, and thus it is an extremely flexible system, adapting to changing realities. The conversion factor is quite simple: fewer clients – less legitimacy of funding, or less funding.

Another system analysed was the legal aid system in Sweden. The Swedish experience is extremely valuable from the point of view of Polish solutions. The Swedish system, as already mentioned, had a rich history of legal aid in its broadest sense, including a period when the country was regarded as the most generous in terms of access to legal aid. It was assumed that there were several paths

---

1 Efficiency understood as involving lawyers in more complicated cases, which makes spending on more expensive lawyers a last resort.

to legal aid for citizens, which often overlapped and actually deterred citizens. This state of affairs made it an extremely expensive system. The Swedish legislator, when choosing to abandon the solutions of the time, decided to base the system of legal aid in its broadest sense on two pillars:

1. compulsory legal insurance; and
2. citizen participation in the cost of legal aid.

The only element that has remained completely free of charge is pre-litigation legal advice provided by attorneys or their assistants. At the same time, as indicated, this is limited in time to 45 minutes. The Swedish legislature has completely abandoned the creation of a separate network of legal aid centres in favour of law firms that provide such assistance. The legal advice service is overseen by the Bar Association. However, an active central body has been introduced to supervise the performance of legal aid in the form of the Legal Aid Board. It examines whether a case qualifies for legal aid, which entails the need for legal representation and significant costs to the state.

The last system analysed was the Ukrainian system. This is certainly the "youngest" of the analysed solutions, which has undergone the toughest test possible – war. It is the system that is most similar to Polish civic counselling, the so-called "primary legal aid". One of the interesting aspects of the Ukrainian system is the existence of a website "https://wiki.legalaid.gov.ua/", which contains extensive information on current issues important to citizens. The site provides instructions within specific categories on how to proceed in selected cases that affect virtually every resident of Ukraine. In addition, it is a system that can easily be expanded, as well as provide citizens' basic needs (dispense hot water, provide outlets for Internet charging), as the last year of Ukrainian reality has proven.

Also of great interest is the frequent holding of informational meetings for citizens, at which issues germane for the functioning of the citizen are discussed, such as receiving subsidies from the state that, for example, reduce the cost of municipal fees. The Ukrainian system is certainly the closest to the Polish system, which makes the Ukrainian experience extremely valuable in improving Polish solutions.

Citizen counselling and pre-litigation legal aid, are elements of direct legal support for citizens, all the more so at a time of an unprecedented number of changes in the law. Moreover, it is citizen counselling and pre-litigation legal aid that should be a source of information for the legislator on the effectiveness of the adopted solutions. At the same time, legal aid in its broadest sense is a specific instrument that requires continuous improvement for its effectiveness.

Looking at the experience of the countries studied, it is impossible to conclude that any of the systems analysed could be fully implementable in Polish conditions. However, this does not exclude the possibility of selecting certain solutions and proposing measures to improve the Polish system. The proposed improvements to legal aid in its broadest sense can be approached from a number of perspectives, but the most important of these, taking into account comparative legal experience, is that of the effectiveness of the system combined with its accessibility on the one hand, and the rationality of spending public funds on the other. With these two key criteria in mind, the authors will propose three options for improving the Polish system.

The first model is that of rationalising spending on legal aid in its broadest sense. It assumes solutions in which civic counselling is abandoned in favour of extended legal aid as is the case, for example, in Sweden or Ukraine. In this way, we avoid a situation in which there is an overlap of legal aid instruments for citizens (i.e. in the Polish system of civic counselling and legal aid, and eliminates the problem of double financing of legal aid in the broader sense), while on the other hand – as the Swedish experience shows – the multiplicity of legal aid instruments leads to the citizen being unable to find himself in the available solutions and is thus less willing to use these services.

Another element is the issue of persons providing legal aid in the broader sense. One should consider the desirability of introducing the Swedish model, in which legal aid is provided in law offices by professional attorneys, particularly in large cities and towns. In Poland, to some extent, the problem lies in smaller municipalities, where the availability of professional legal services is difficult. However, there is nothing to prevent interested persons who meet the requirements for using the free legal aid service from taking advantage of it anywhere. To some extent, such a solution could even improve access to legal aid centres in the broad sense. We are of the opinion that professional attorneys and their trainees should be included in the provision of this service. On the other hand, the provision of legal aid, in the more literal sense of the term, by attorneys, legal advisers and trainee attorneys or legal advisers, will allow the use of pre-existing network of premises in the form of law offices within which they operate.[2] We believe that such assistance should be completely free of charge but, on the other

2 In the case of trainees, this solution should be combined with the provisions governing the practice of the profession of advocate or legal adviser, according to which the trainee is entitled to be a substitute before a district court, a regional court, an appeal court, etc. after completing a certain period of training.

hand, limited in time to legal advice (following the example of the countries studied, to a maximum of 45 minutes). This will make it possible to provide legal aid for minor cases and separate cases that require more involvement and financial outlay on the part of the state.

Another element within the optimal model is the creation of a central body to oversee the provision of legal aid. This will improve the functioning of the system as such and unify it, while at the same time it will be a body, on the model of Swedish solutions, overseeing the level of legal advice provided. In Poland, to some extent, this role is fulfilled by the Ministry of Justice. However, the creation of an independent institution established only to provide this service should be considered.

One of the key aspects of this model, is the introduction of compulsory legal insurance for selected categories of cases, especially those requiring judicial involvement. Their determination can be a product of a number of factors, such as at least the frequency of specific cases or their social importance. Following the model of Swedish solutions, these could be real estate disputes in the first instance.

Next, it is necessary to consider the need for a free mediator within this model. The legislator in many places seeks to create the possibility of settling cases amicably, in order to relieve the burden on the courts. In this regard, it seems appropriate to introduce the free assistance of a mediator who can lead to a settlement in cases where this is permissible

It is also reasonable to introduce a solution for a person's participation in the costs of legal aid, but at the court stage in particular in civil cases. This participation may be purely symbolic and relate to the value of the dispute or appeal, depending on the stage of the proceedings at which legal aid is provided.

The second proposed model is similar to the one indicated above, with one difference in the form of waiving the beneficiary's participation in the cost of legal aid.

The third model – also based on the first – assumes that legal insurance will be waived and legal aid cost-sharing will be waived. The assumption is that free pre-litigation legal aid will be available, which will actually include citizen counselling and pre-litigation legal assistance. This service will be provided by professional attorneys or their trainees. In any case that has so-called settlement suitability, the free assistance of a mediator will be available. Additionally, in addition to the central body overseeing legal aid, there may be provincial or district legal aid centres, which may organise training for legal aid providers, as well as the preparation of videos with information for citizens on how they can solve a specific legal problem.

Somewhat in addition to all the models, deep consideration should be given to the creation of a unified information website, where citizens can receive information before going to the legal aid centre, which in many cases may be sufficient. The model in this case is certainly the Ukrainian system. The website created is divided, as already mentioned, into specific branches of law and includes a synthetic description and instructions on how to proceed. For example, going to https://wiki.legalaid.gov.ua/ the first thing you see is the category "Family Law"; after clicking on this an alphabetical list of case categories appears, for example, "Large family – certificates and reliefs" or "State registration of abandoned or found child".[3]

In the Polish context, this information is, of course, available on the Internet, but it is often difficult to find and scattered over many websites. The collection and continuous expansion of information on a single site will allow the creation of a single place containing information on the most current issues and, it is assumed, will lead to a situation in which people seek legal assistance in complex cases.

3 Source: https://wiki.legalaid.gov.ua/ndex.php/Категорія:Сімейне_право.

Summary

The study presents solutions for free pre-litigation legal aid in comparative terms. In addition to Polish regulations, the regulations of the following countries were analysed:

(a) Sweden (as an example of a developed democracy with rich experience in providing free legal aid);
(b) Ukraine (as an example of an "emerging democracy"); and
(c) The United Kingdom of Great Britain and Northern Ireland (as an example of a country with a *common law* system).

The research suggests that there is no uniform approach to guaranteeing free pre-litigation legal aid, as well as to the understanding of civic counselling. In the solutions analysed in Great Britain and Northern Ireland civic counselling is understood in the strict sense of the word, and in Sweden and Ukraine it is only possible to identify institutions that perform the functions of civic counselling in the broader sense only to some extent. In Sweden, legal advice is highlighted, whereas in Ukraine it is the institution of primary legal aid.

An analysis of the solutions leads to the conclusion that the subject matter of the cases under this assistance also differs. Citizens' advice in Great Britain and Northern Ireland is the broadest (it includes both legal aid and civic counselling). A fairly wide range of assistance is provided in Ukraine. The narrowest scope of assistance is in the Swedish system.

There is also a lack of a unified approach to the organisation of the provision of free legal aid (civic or legal advice). It should be emphasised that there are institutions (entities) providing this assistance (Ukraine, as well as Sweden), which on the one hand have permanent funding from the state (or local government bodies), while on the other hand, in the United Kingdom, this assistance depends on periodic grants, subsidies and donations. Evaluating the British solutions (both as to the method of financing and the rather elaborate organisation), one can note the greater risk in the provision of this assistance. The example of Sweden indicates that significant financial difficulties determined the reform of the system of free legal aid.

It should also be emphasised that not all assistance is free of charge in all countries. That is the case in the UK and Ukraine, while in Sweden, as a rule, partial financial participation of the citizen in practically every type of legal advice has been introduced. Hence, totally free of charge is the exception. Ukrainian solutions, on the other hand, due to the short period in existence of the constructions analysed, illustrate an interesting development, and with skilful management they can become a model.

In light of the findings, it should be concluded that building a system of free legal aid in the broader sense (including its various stages, especially pre-litigation and court), including civic counselling, or legal advice, is a challenge for state bodies. The pre-1993 Swedish and British experience shows that the system of assistance supporting the protection of people's rights through legal aid should be constantly monitored and improved, especially from the point of view of its financial viability. This is particularly important in the face of the economic crisis, where, on the one hand, there is a need for special legal assistance to people in difficult life (financial) situations, while on the other is the need to ensure a state of budgetary balance. In this state of affairs, the most rational solution remains the introduction of some objective criteria for access to this type of public service. A fairly clear criterion is the income of the individual. The idea is that free legal aid should be addressed to those who need it most in order to realise the principle of social justice and the right to a court.

A properly functioning legal aid system (taking into account both convention and constitutional standards for the protection of human rights) can have a positive impact on reducing the number of complaints to the courts. Hence, it is important that legal regulations (including, in particular, those relating to the system of free legal aid) promote the resolution of conflict cases without involving the judiciary (and thus generating court costs[1]), but strengthen the system of protection of individual rights and encourage the use of mediation.[2] However, the individual should be provided with opportunities to receive information about his/her freedoms, rights and procedural rules for asserting them at the judicial level (in civil procedure, criminal procedure or administrative court proceedings). Hence, pre-litigation legal aid can be an element in the effective realisation of the right to a court (at its initial stage – activation). Such an understanding of free pre-litigation legal aid can be derived directly or indirectly from a

1 See also e.g. Flaga-Gruszyńska, *Idea*, p. 56.

2 Compare: M. Araszkiewicz, K. Płeszka, *Pojęcie alternatywnego rozwiązywania sporów*, [in:] *Mediacja. Teoria, normy, praktyka*, red. K. Płeszka, J. Czapska, M. Araszkiewicz, M. Pękala, Warszawa 2017, pp. 45–157, zob. też interesujące rozważania na temat pomocy prawnej: M. Araszkiewicz, *Nieodpłatna pomoc prawna – przegląd badań i materiałów z zakresu ekonomicznej analizy prawa*, Warszawa 2012, source: https://www.ekonomiaspoleczna.gov.pl/download/files/PPIO/Przeglad_badan_dot_pomocy_prawnej.pdf (access: 22.12.2022 r.).

number of international norms, in particular: the Convention on Human Rights, the Convention on the Rights of Persons with Disabilities, the Convention on the Rights of the Child, the Convention against Torture and Other Cruel, Inhuman or Degrading Treatment or Punishment, the Council of Europe Convention on Action against Trafficking in Human Beings, the Council of Europe Convention on Preventing and Combating Violence against Women and Domestic Violence. The *soft law of* the Council of Europe also leads to such conclusions.

The system of legal aid (including at the pre-litigation stage), as a public service, should respond to social expectations and, therefore, be structured in such a way that as many people as possible who are in a difficult life situation can benefit from this assistance. There is no doubt that one of the needs of society is to create effective solutions to ensure access to the law in the broadest sense. Implementation of this task requires coordination with other public policies. In this regard, it is possible to draw on the experience of countries which are known for their effective social policies in the field of mechanisms of access to the law. The idea of allowing remote advice deserves praise, but requires further changes in the means of its provision.[3] Efforts should be made to simplify the system of free legal aid, including, to the extent possible, the creation of mechanisms for the implementation of this service remotely using the potential of trainee attorneys and trainee legal advisers in Poland.

The process of working out optimal solutions should include, on the one hand, representatives of public administration bodies, and on the other, representatives of the professional associations of attorneys and legal advisers and non-governmental organisations. In particular, the meetings of the Council for Free Legal Aid, Free Civic Counselling and Legal Education serve as a platform for the development of solutions. The activities of this body focused, in particular, on working out compromise solutions, with the broadest possible support of the communities on amendments to the law on free legal aid, aimed at increasing the availability and efficiency of services for those in need of assistance. It is worth noting that the deliberations were attended by, among others: representatives of the Joint Commission of the Government and Local Self-Government, the Supreme Bar Council, the National Council of Legal Advisers, NGOs and government administration. This type of forum for the exchange of experience should be evaluated positively, in terms of the implementation of the concept of so-called responsive administration, adapting to the needs of society.

3 See also: Winczorek, *Pandemia COVID-19*, p. 59.

Bibliography

Collective works

Araszkiewicz M., *Nieodpłatna pomoc prawna – przegląd badań i materiałów z zakresu ekonomicznej analizy prawa*, Warszawa 2012.

Araszkiewicz M., Płeszka K., *Pojęcie alternatywnego rozwiązywania sporów*, [in:] *Mediacja. Teoria, normy, praktyka*, red. K. Płeszka, J. Czapska, M. Araszkiewicz, M. Pękala, Warszawa 2017.

Araszkiewicz M., *Technologie informacyjne a nieodpłatna pomoc prawna*, Warszawa 2015.

Augustyniak M., Moll T., *Ustawa o samorządzie gminnym. Komentarz*, red. B. Dolnicki, Warszawa 2021, LEX, commentary on art. 7.

Banaszak B., *Prawo konstytucyjne*, Warszawa 2015.

Bandarzewski K., *Udzielanie nieodpłatnej pomocy prawnej jako zadanie zlecone powiatowi*, [in:] *Charakter i konstrukcja zadań samorządu terytorialnego*, red. M. Stec, S. Płażek Warszawa 2017.

Barankiewicz T., *Etyczne treści prawa do dobrej administracji*, [in:] *System Prawa Administracyjnego*, t. 13, *Etyka urzędnicza i etyka służby publicznej*, red. R. Hauser, Z. Niewiadomski, A. Wróbel, Warszawa 2016.

Bartnik A. S., Kowalska K. J., *Nieodpłatna pomoc prawna*, Warszawa 2019.

Biernat S., *Czy Karta Praw Podstawowych Unii Europejskiej obowiązuje w Polsce?*, [in:] *Państwo prawa i prawo karne. Księga Jubileuszowa Profesora Andrzeja Zolla*, t. 1, red. P. Kardas, T. Sroka, W. Wróbel, Warszawa 2012.

Bisztyga A., *Prawo do rozpatrzenia sprawy w rozsądnym terminie. Nowe działania: ADR, e-sąd*, [in:] *Transformacja systemów wymiaru sprawiedliwości w państwach Europy Środkowej i wschodniej w latach 1990–2010*, red. J. Jaskiernia, Toruń 2011.

Blicharz J., *Komentarz do ustawy o działalności pożytku publicznego i wolontariacie*, [in:] *Ustawa o działalności pożytku publicznego i wolontariacie. Ustawa o spółdzielniach socjalnych*. Komentarz, Warszawa 2012.

Całkiewicz D., Rotkiewicz A., *Prawo pomocy jako gwarancja prawa do sądu dla najuboższych w świetle prawa międzynarodowego i unijnego oraz w przepisach ustawy – Prawo o postępowaniu sądowoadministracyjnym*, [in:] *Dziesięć lat polskich doświadczeń w Unii Europejskiej. Problemy prawnoadministracyjne*, red. J. Sługocki, t. 2, Warszawa 2014.

Chmielnicki P., *Pochodzenie, tworzenie i efektywność prawa*, Warszawa 2014.

Chmielnicki P., *System (bez)prawnej pomocy, czyli jak rząd Ewy Kopacz poradził sobie z nadprodukcją prawników*, [in:] *Fenomen prawa administracyjnego. Księga jubileuszowa Profesora Jana Zimmermana*, red. W. Jakimowicz, M. Krawczyk, I. Niżnik-Dobosz, Warszawa 2019.

Czepek J., *Zobowiązania pozytywne państwa w sferze praw człowieka pierwszej generacji na tle Europejskiej Konwencji Praw Człowieka*, Olsztyn 2014.

Czernicki F., *Dostęp do nieodpłatnej przedsądowej pomocy prawnej w Polsce*, [in:] *Prawo wobec problemów społecznych. Księga jubileuszowa Profesor Eleonory Zielińskiej*, red. B. Namysłowska-Gabrysiak, K. Syroka-Marczewska, A. Walczak-Żochowska, Warszawa 2016.

Dudek D., *Czy zawsze zmiana prawa jest koniecznym remedium na każde naruszenie praw człowieka?*, [in:] *IX Seminarium Warszawskie. Dysfunkcje polskiego prawa – jak poprawić system środków prawnych w Polsce?*, Warszawa 2016, source: https://www.gov.pl/web/dyplomacja/seminaria-warszawskie-publikacje (access: 21.11.2020).

Flaga-Gieruszyńska K., *Idea pomocy prawnej z urzędu w postępowaniu cywilnym*, [in:] *Aequitas sequitur legem. Księga Jubileuszowa z okazji 75. urodzin Profesora Andrzeja Zielińskiego*, red. K. Flaga-Gieruszyńska, G. Jędrejek, Warszawa 2014.

Florczak W., *Nieodpłatna pomoc prawna w Polsce. Systemowa analiza interdyscyplinarna*, Kraków 2021.

Florczak-Wątor M., *Horyzontalny wymiar praw konstytucyjnych*, Kraków 2014.

Florczak-Wątor M., *Podstawy prawne obowiązków ochronnych państwa w Konstytucji RP*, [in:] *Ochrona praw człowieka. Zagadnienia praktyczne*, red. A. Hauser, M. Urbaniak, Poznań 2019.

Florczak-Wątor M., *Rola sądów i trybunałów w kształtowaniu koncepcji horyzontalnego działania praw jednostki*, [in:] *Sądy i trybunały wobec problemu horyzontalnego działania praw jednostki*, red. M. Florczak-Wątor, Kraków 2015.

Garlicki L., *Konwencja o Ochronie Praw Człowieka i Podstawowych Wolności*, t. 1, *Komentarz do artykułów 1–18*, red. L. Garlicki, Warszawa 2010.

Garlicki L., Wojtyczek K., *Komentarz do art. 77 Konstytucji RP*, [in:] *Konstytucja Rzeczypospolitej Polskiej. Komentarz*, red. L. Garlicki, M. Zubik, t. 2, Warszawa 2016.

Gołaczyński J., Krzywonos A., *Prawo do sądu*, [in:] *Prawa i wolności obywatelskie w Konstytucji RP*, red. B. Banaszak, A. Preisner, Warszawa 2002.

Goss, R., *The Undermining of Article 6 ECHR*, [in:] *European Yearbook on Human Rights*, ed. P. Czech, L. Heschl, K. Lukas, M. Nowak, G. Oberleitner, 2019.

Grabenwarter C. (ed.), *European Convention on Human Rights*, 2023.

Granat M., *Prawo konstytucyjne. Pytania i odpowiedzi*, Warszawa 2019.

Heuman L., *Rättshjälp och pilotfall*, SvJT 1983.

Hofmański P., Wróbel A., *Komentarz do art. 6 EKPCz*, [in:] *Konwencja o Ochronie Praw Człowieka i Podstawowych Wolności. Komentarz do artykułów 1–18*, red. L. Garlicki, t. 1, Warszawa 2010.

Izdebski H., *Zasada dobrej administracji i prawo do dobrej administracji w świetle standardów Rady Europy*, [in:] *60 lat Rady Europy. Tworzenie i stosowanie standardów prawnych*, red. H. Machińska, Warszawa 2009.

Jabłoński M., *Prawo do nieodpłatnej pomocy prawnej jako „element treści konstytucyjnego prawa do sądu" – uwagi na te postanowień ustawy z 5 sierpnia 2015 r. o nieodpłatnej pomocy prawnej oraz edukacji prawnej*, [in:] *Ochrona praw człowieka. Zagadnienia praktyczne*, red. A. Hauser, M. Urbaniak, Poznań 2019.

Joseph S., Castan M., *The International Covenant on Civil and Political Rights: Cases, Materials*, Oxford University Press 2013.

Jan Paweł II, *Nauczanie społeczne*, t. 3, Warszawa 1984.

Jaskiernia J., *Funkcje Konstytucji RP w dobie integracji europejskiej i radykalnych przemian politycznych*, Toruń 2020.

Jaskiernia J., *Rada Europy jako organizacja międzynarodowa kreująca i oddziaływująca na implementację standardów demokratycznych*, [in:] *Rada Europy a przemiany demokratyczne w państwach Europy Środkowej i Wschodniej w latach 1989–2009*, red. J. Jaskiernia, Warszawa 2010.

Kaczocha M., *Ustawa o nieodpłatnej pomocy prawnej oraz edukacji prawnej. Komentarz*, LEX/el. 2016.

Kędzia Z., Hernandez-Połczyńska A. (ed.), *Międzynarodowy Pakt Praw Gospodarczych, Socjalnych i Kulturalnych. Komentarz*, Warszawa 2018.

Klich A., *Idea pomocy prawnej w sprawach cywilnych a działalność klinik prawa*, [in:] *Aequitas sequitur legem. Księga Jubileuszowa z okazji 75. urodzin Profesora Andrzeja Zielińskiego*, red. K. Flaga-Gieruszyńska, G. Jędrejek, Warszawa 2014.

Kruszyński P., *Zasada prawa do obrony w świetle orzecznictwa Europejskiego Trybunału Praw Człowieka w Strasburgu – zagadnienia wybrane*, [in:] *Gaudium in litteris est. Księga Jubileuszowa ofiarowana Pani Profesor Genowefie Rejman z okazji osiemdziesiątych urodzin*, Warszawa 2005.

Kurowski M., *Kodeks postępowania karnego*, t. 1, *Komentarz aktualizowany*, red. D. Świecki, LEX 2021, komentarz do art. 180.

Kuta T., *Funkcje współczesnej administracji i sposoby ich realizacji*, Wrocław 1992.

Lipowicz I., *O mądre prawo i wrażliwe państwo*, Warszawa 2013.

McDermont M., *Citizens Advice in austere times*, [in:] *Advising in austerity. Reflections on challenging times for advice agencies*, ed. S. Kirwan, Advising in austerity, Bristol, 2017.

D. McGoldrick, *The Human Rights Committee. Its Role in the Development of the International Covenant on Civil and Political Rights*, 2nd edition, Oxford 1994.

Michalski M., Kotowski A., Wiśniewski R., Dąbrowska J., Syryt A., Zarzecki M., *Normatywny model współpracy samorządu terytorialnego z organizacjami pozarządowymi. Wybrane zagadnienia*, red. A. Kotowski, S. Wijas, Warszawa 2021.

Mik C., *Teoria obowiązków pozytywnych państw-stron traktatów w dziedzinie praw człowieka na przykładzie Europejskiej Konwencji Praw Człowieka*, [in:] *Księga Jubileuszowa Profesora Tadeusza Jasudowicza*, red. J. Białocerkiewicz, M. Balcerzak, A. Czeczko-Durlak, Toruń 2004, pp. 257–276.

Morawska E. H., *Zobowiązania pozytywne państw-stron Konwencji o ochronie praw człowieka i podstawowych wolności*, Warszawa 2016.

Motyka K., *Prawa człowieka. Wprowadzenie. Wybór źródeł*, Lublin 2004.

Vogiatzis N., *Interpreting the Right to Interpretation under Article 6(3)(e) ECHR: A Cautious Evolution in the Jurisprudence of the European Court of Human Rights?, Human Rights Law Review*, [in:] *European Yearbook on Human Rights*, ed. P. Czech, L. Heschl, K. Lukas, M. Nowak, G. Oberleitner, 2019.

Nitecki S., *Solidarność a pomoc społeczna*, [in:] *Państwo solidarne*, red. A. Łabno, Warszawa 2018.

Niżnik-Dobosz I., *Ustawa o wychowaniu w trzeźwości i przeciwdziałaniu alkoholizmowi. Komentarz*, red. M. Koszowski, I. Niżnik-Dobosz, Warszawa 2020.

Nowacki J., *Sprawiedliwość legalna a „wymiar sprawiedliwości"*, [in:] *Współczesne problemy procesu karnego i wymiaru sprawiedliwości. Księga ku czci Profesora Kazimierza Marszała*, red. P. Hofmański, K. Zgryzek, Katowice 2003.

Nowicki M. A., *Komentarz do art. 14 EKPCz*, [in:] *Wokół Konwencji Europejskiej. Komentarz do Europejskiej Konwencji Praw Człowieka*, red. M. A. Nowicki, Warszawa 2017.

Nowicki M. A., *Prawo do rzetelnego procesu sądowego*, [in:] *Europejski Trybunał Praw Człowieka. Wybór orzeczeń*, red. M. A. Nowicki, Warszawa 2013.

Nowicki M. A., *Wokół Konwencji Europejskiej. Komentarz do Europejskiej Konwencji Praw Człowieka*, Warszawa 2017.

Paxford B., *Komentarz do art. 2*, [in:] *Ustawa o nieodpłatnej pomocy prawnej oraz edukacji prawnej. Komentarz*, red. B. Paxford, R. Rynkun-Werner, M. Wasylkowska-Michór, Warszawa 2016.

Płażek S., *Nowe usługi powiatu w zakresie nieodpłatnej pomocy prawnej*, [in:] *Działalność gospodarcza jednostek samorządu terytorialnego. Dopuszczalność i granice jej prowadzenia*, red. M. Stec, M. Mączyński, Warszawa 2016.

Ploszka A., *Publicznoprawny status jednostki skrajnie ubogiej*, Warszawa 2019.

Przybysz P., *Prawo do sądu w sprawach administracyjnych*, [in:] *Prawo administracyjne w okresie transformacji ustrojowej*, red. E. Knosala, A. Matan, G. Łaszczyca, Kraków 1999.

Przywora B., *Europejska Karta Społeczna jako wzorzec kontroli prawa w świetle orzecznictwa Trybunału Konstytucyjnego*, [in:] *Ochrona praw człowieka w Europie. Aksjologia, instytucje, nowe wyzwania, praktyka*, red. J. Jaskiernia, K. Spryszak, t. 3, Toruń 2017.

Przywora B., *Normatywny model przedsądowej nieodpłatnej pomocy prawnej w Polsce*, Warszawa 2019.

Przywora B., Wróbel A., *Status prawny sędziego w Królestwie Szwecji*, [in:] *Status prawny sędziego Państwa europejskie*, t. 1, red. B. Przywora, Warszawa 2019.

Przywora B., *Z problematyki wykonywania mandatu posła i senatora - kilka refleksji*, [in:] *Ustroje - prawa człowieka - bezpieczeństwo - integracja europejska. Księga Jubileuszowa z okazji 70 urodzin Profesora Jerzego Jaskierni*, red. R. M. Czarny, Ł. Baratyński, P. Ramiączek, K. Spryszak, t. 1, Toruń 2020.

Rainey B., McCormick P., Ovey C., *The European Convention on Human Rights*, 2021.

Reiling A. D., *Technology for Justice: How Information Technology Can Support Judicial Reform*, Leiden 2009.

Sarnecki P., *Komentarz do art. 9 i 45 Konstytucji RP*, [in:] *Konstytucja Rzeczypospolitej Polskiej. Komentarz*, t. 1, red. L. Garlicki, M. Zubik, Warszawa 2016.

Schabas W. A., *The European Convention on Human Rights: A Commentary*, 2015.

Schoultz I., *Legal Aid in Sweden*, [in:] *Outsourcing Legal Aid in the Nordic Welfare States*, red. O. H. Rønning, O. Hammerslev, Lund 2018.

Sokolewicz W., Zubik M., *Konstytucja RP*, t. 1, *Komentarz do art. 1–86*, red. M. Safjan, L. Bosek, Warszawa 2016.

Spryszak K., *Uniwersalne standardy z obszaru „miękkiego prawa"*, [in:] *Współczesne wyzwania państwa i prawa. Księga jubileuszowa z okazji 45-lecia pracy naukowej profesora Jerzego Jaskierni*, red. Ł. Baratyński, P. Ramiączek, K. Spryszak Toruń 2017.

Staszczyk P., Art. 1, [in:] *Ustawa o działalności pożytku publicznego i o wolontariacie. Komentarz*, Warszawa 2022.

Świątkowski A. M., *Karta Praw Społecznych Rady Europy*, Warszawa 2006.

Trela J., *Prawo o adwokaturze. Komentarz*, red. P. Kruszyński, Warszawa 2016, LEX, komentarz do art. 77 pr. adw.

Trociuk S., *Pomoc prawna dla osób ubogich jako forma zapewnienia skutecznego dostępu do krajowego i europejskiego wymiaru sprawiedliwości*, [in:] *Dostęp obywateli do europejskiego wymiaru sprawiedliwości*, red. H. Izdebski, H. Machińska, Warszawa 2005.

Tuleja P., *Stosowanie Konstytucji RP w świetle zasady jej nadrzędności. Wybrane problemy*, Kraków 2003.

Waltoś S., *Zasada w polskim procesie karnym*, [in:] *System Prawa Karnego Procesowego*, red. P. Hofmański, t. 3, cz. 1, *Zasady procesu karnego*, red. P. Wiliński, Warszawa 2014.

Wąsek-Wiaderek M., *Prawo oskarżonego do posiadania obrońcy w świetle orzecznictwa Europejskiego Trybunału Praw Człowieka*, [in:] *Studia i analizy Sądu Najwyższego*, red. K. Ślebzak, t. 6, Warszawa 2012.

Wieruszewski R. (ed.), *Międzynarodowy Pakt Praw Obywatelskich (Osobistych) i Politycznych. Komentarz*, Warszawa 2012.

Wieruszewski R., Stupak P., *Postępowanie o nadanie statusu uchodźcy w Polsce*, [in:] *Ochrona praw człowieka. Zagadnienia praktyczne*, red. A. Hauser, M. Urbaniak, Poznań 2019.

Wiliński P., Karlik P., *Komentarz do art. 42 Konstytucji RP*, [in:] *Konstytucja RP*, t. 1, *Komentarz. Art. 1–86*, red. M. Safjan, L. Bosek, Warszawa 2016.

Winczorek J., *Dostęp do prawa. Ujęcie socjologiczne*, Warszawa 2019.

Wójtowicz K., *Komentarz do art. 9 RP*, [in:] *Konstytucja RP*, t. 1, *Komentarz do art. 1–86*, red. M. Safjan, L. Bosek, Warszawa 2016.

Wróbel A. (ed.), *Karta Praw Podstawowych Unii Europejskiej. Komentarz*, Warszawa 2020.

Wróbel A., *Preambuła*, [in:] *Karta Praw Podstawowych Unii Europejskiej. Komentarz*, red. A. Wróbel, Warszawa 2020.

Wujczyk M., *Europejski Komitet Praw Społecznych Rady Europy jako ponadpaństwowy organ ochrony praw człowieka*, [in:] *Instytucje ochrony praw człowieka*, red. B. Szmulik, A. Pogłodek, B. Przywora, Warszawa 2014.

Zoll A., *Dostęp do informacji prawnej jako prawo obywatelskie*, [in:] *Informacja prawna a prawa obywatela. Konferencja z okazji XXXV-lecia informatyki prawniczej w Polsce i XV-lecia Systemu Informacji Prawnej LEX, Gdańsk, 19–20 czerwca 2006*, red. K. Grajewski, J. Warylewski, Warszawa 2006.

Zweigert K., Kötz H., *Introduction to Comparative Law*, New York 1998.

Данилевська Ю.О., Павлик Л.В., Петрович З.З., Цмоць У.О., *Право особи на безоплатну правову допомогу*, Львів 2018.

Тацій В.Я. (ed.), *Конституція України. Науково-практичний коментар*, Харків 2011.

Articles

Banaszak B., *Zalety i wady Karty Praw Podstawowych Unii Europejskiej*, „Przegląd Sejmowy" 2008, nr 2 (85).

Barcik J., Srogosz T., *Prawo dostępu do adwokata w Polsce w świetle dyrektywy 2013/48/UE*, „Palestra" 2015, nr 7–8.

Bisztyga A., *Europejska Konwencja Praw Człowieka a Karta Praw Podstawowych Unii Europejskiej – stan kompatybilności czy konkurencyjności?*, „Przegląd Prawa Konstytucyjnego" 2011, nr 3.

Chavan A., *Mobile strategies for legal services*, "Harvard Journal of Law & Technology" 2012, nr 26.

Chmielnicki P., *Metodyka badań nad materialnymi źródłami prawa. Cz. 1. Podstawy*, „Przegląd Prawa Publicznego" 2012, nr 3.

Chmielnicki P., *Metodyka badań nad materialnymi źródłami prawa. Cz. 2. Uzasadnienie i objaśnienia poszczególnych faz badań*, „Przegląd Prawa Publicznego" 2012, nr 4.

Czeszejko-Sochacki Z., *Prawo do sądu w świetle Konstytucji Rzeczypospolitej Polskiej (ogólna charakterystyka)*, „Państwo i Prawo" 1997, z. 11–12.

Daniluk D., *Nieodpłatne poradnictwo obywatelskie w świetle ustawy o nieodpłatnej pomocy prawnej, nieodpłatnym poradnictwie obywatelskim oraz edukacji prawnej. Wymiar teoretyczny i praktyczny*, „Przegląd Prawa Publicznego" 2022, nr 10.

Daniluk D., *Świadczenie nieodpłatnego poradnictwa obywatelskiego przez radcę prawnego lub adwokata a obowiązek zachowania tajemnicy zawodowej i unikania konfliktu interesów*, „Radca Prawny. Zeszyty Naukowe" 2022, nr 1(30).

Daniluk D., *Zmiany regulacji prawnych dotyczących nieodpłatnej pomocy prawnej i nieodpłatnego poradnictwa obywatelskiego w związku z pandemią wirusa SARS-CoV-2*, „Przegląd Legislacyjny" 2022, nr 1.

Florczak-Wątor M., *Konstytucja jako źródło obowiązków państwa w stosunku do obywatela*, „Ruch Prawniczy, Ekonomiczny I Socjologiczny" 2018, t. 80, nr 1.

Gil-Bazo M.T., *The Charter of Fundamental Rights of the European Union and the Right to be Granted Asylum in the Union's Law*, Refugee Survey Quarterly, Volume 27, Issue 3, 2008, Pages 33–52.

Hałub O., *Konstytucyjne gwarancje prawa do nieodpłatnej pomocy prawnej na etapie przedsądowym*, „Forum Prawnicze" 2016, nr 4.

Hough B. R., *Let's not make it worse. Issues to consider in adopting new technology*, "Harvard Journal of Law & Technology" 2012, nr 26.

Kirwan S., McDermont M., Clarke J., *Imagining and practicing citizenship in austere times: the work of Citizens Advice*, "Citizenship Studies" 2016, nr 20, z. 6–7.

Korman Sloviter D., *Let's Look at Citizens Advice Bureaux*, "American Bar Association Journal" 1979, nr 65(4).

Kokott J, Sobbotta Ch., *The Charter of Fundamental Rights of the European Union after Lisbon*, EUI AEL, 2010/06, Distinguished Lectures of the Academy.

Lipowicz I., *Stan ochrony praw człowieka z perspektywy Rzecznika Praw Obywatelskich*, „Ruch Prawniczy, Ekonomiczny i Socjologiczny" 2014, z. 2.

Menéndez A. J., *Chartering Europe: Legal Status and Policy Implications of the Charter of Fundamental Rights of the European Union*, JCMS: Journal of Common Market Studies, 2002 40: 471-490;

Muther P. S., *Reform of Legal Aid in Sweden*, "International Lawyer" 2020, nr 9(3), source: https://core.ac.uk/download/pdf/216914158.pdf (access: 17.12.2020).

Maciejko W., [in:] W. Maciejko, P. Zaborniak, *Ustawa o pomocy społecznej. Komentarz*, Warszawa 2013, LEX, komentarz do art. 19 u.p.s.

Podkowik J., *Wymogi europejskiej Konwencji o ochronie praw człowieka i podstawowych wolności dotyczące sądownictwa wojskowego*, „Przegląd Sejmowy" 2010, nr 3(98).

Przywora B., *Free legal assistance as an instrument in protecting the right of foreigners in the Republic of Poland – a contributions to the discussion*, „Annuals of The Administration and Law" 2020, XX, z. 1.

Rabinovich-Einy O., Katsh E., *Access to digital justice: Fair and efficient processes for the Modern Age*, "Cardozo Journal of Conflict Resolution" 2016, nr 16.

Rexer L., Malone P., *Overcoming barriers to adoption of effective technology strategies for improving access to justice*, "Harvard Journal of Law & Technology" 2012, nr 26.

Rząsa G., *Konstytucyjne aspekty pomocy prawnej udzielanej osobom ubogim*, „Przegląd Legislacyjny" 2005, nr 3–4.

Stefaniuk M., *Społeczna potrzeba nieodpłatnej pomocy prawnej – beneficjenci regulacji ustawowej*, „Studia Iuridica Lublinensia" 2016, nr XXV, z. 3.

Symonides J., *Powszechna Deklaracja Praw Człowieka (po 60 latach od jej przyjęcia)*, „Państwo i Prawo" 2008, nr 12.

Uziębło P. J., [in:] K. Grajewski, J. Stelina, P. J. Uziębło, *Komentarz do ustawy o wykonywaniu mandatu posła i senatora*, Warszawa 2014, LEX, komentarz do art. 24.

Velicogna M., Steigenga E., Taal S., Schmidt A., *Connecting EU jurisdictions: Exploring how to open justice across member states through ICT*, "Social Science Computer Review" 2008.

Wegner J., Wróblewski B., *Prawo jednostki do nieodpłatnej pomocy prawnej*, „Przegląd Prawa Publicznego" 2021, nr 6.

Wieruszewski R., *Rola i znaczenie Karty Praw Podstawowych Unii Europejskiej dla ochrony praw człowieka*, „Przegląd Sejmowy" 2008, nr 2(85).

Winczorek J., *O potrzebie badań empirycznych nad dostępem do prawa*, „Państwo i Prawo" 2016, nr 12.

Winczorek J., *Pandemia COVID-19 a dostęp do prawa. Polska na tle wyników badania międzynarodowego*, „Państwo i Prawo" 2020, nr 12.

Winczorek J., *Public interest and access to justice: A liminal analysis*, „Archiwum Filozofii Prawa i Filozofii Społecznej" 2020, nr 3.

Wyrozumska A., *Znaczenie prawne zmiany statusy Karty Praw Podstawowych Unii Europejskiej w Traktacie Lizbońskim oraz Protokołu polsko-brytyjskiego*, „Przegląd Sejmowy" 2008, nr 2(85).

Zucker M., *The British "Citizens' Advice Bureaus"*, "Social Service Review" 1950, nr 24(1).

Zucker M., *Citizens' Advice Bureaus: The British Way*, "Social Work" 1965, nr 10(4).

Гець О., Історичний та сучасний погляди на надання безоплатної правової допомоги адвокатами, Юриспреденція: теорія і практика 2011, № 11.

Сербіна А., Надання безоплатної правової допомоги органами місцевого самоврядування, Місцеве самоврядування–2017,–№ 12, source: https://i.factor.ua/ukr/journals/ms/2017/december/issue-12/article-32589.html, (access: 20.11.2020).

Струкова К., *Особливості організації надання безоплатної правової допомоги недержавними суб'єктами*, Актуальні проблеми правознавства. Випуск 2 (10). 2017 р.

Opinions, expert opinions, reports

Barendrecht M., *Rechtwijzer: Why Online Supported Dispute Resolution is Hard to Implement*, International Legal Aid Group Conference, 14–16.06.2017.

Fisher G., *Advice on Everything. A History of the Citizens Advice Service in Harrow, 1939–2009*, source: https://citizensadvice.citizensadvice.org.uk/harrow_cab_history.pdf (access: 24.11.2020).

Konieczko K., *Opinia do ustawy o nieodpłatnej pomocy prawnej oraz edukacji prawnej (druk nr 962)*, Kancelaria Senatu, Biuro Legislacyjne, 9 lipca 2015 r., https://www.senat.gov.pl/gfx/senat/userfiles/_public/k8/dokumenty/opinie/079/o/962.pdf (dostęp: 24 czerwca 2022 r.).

Konieczko K., *Opinia do ustawy o zmianie ustawy o nieodpłatnej pomocy prawnej oraz edukacji prawnej oraz niektórych innych ustaw (druk nr 865)*, 26 czerwca 2018 r., Kancelaria Senatu, Biuro Legislacyjne, https://www.senat.gov.pl/gfx/senat/pl/senatekspertyzy/4743/plik/865o.pdf (dostęp: 24 czerwca 2022 r.).

Opinia Krajowej Rady Sądownictwa z 16.01.2015 r. w przedmiocie projektu ustawy o nieodpłatnej pomocy prawnej i informacji prawnej, pp. 1–2, source: https://www.adwokatura.pl/admin/wgrane_pliki/file-opiniakrspomoc-10974.pdf (access: 02.07.2022).

Peisert A., Schimanek T., Winiarska A., Waszak M. (ed.), *Poradnictwo prawne i obywatelskie w Polsce: stan obecny i wizje przyszłości*, Warszawa 2013.

Przywora B., Wróbel A., *Analiza prawnoporównawcza sposobów finansowania oraz metod weryfikacji jakości systemu pomocy prawnej i poradnictwa obywatelskiego na tle wybranych państw europejskich*, Warszawa 2022.

Przywora B., Wróbel A., *Poradnictwo obywatelskie w świetle badań prawnoporównawczych*, Warszawa 2020.

Schimanek T., *Możliwości wsparcia bezpłatnego poradnictwa obywatelskiego i prawnego przez samorządy lokalne*, source: http://www.obywateliprawo.isp.org.pl/files/cke/Moliwoci....pdf (access: 12.11.2020).

Waszczuk-Napiórkowska J., *Opinia prawna dotycząca projektu ustawy o nieodpłatnej pomocy prawnej, nieodpłatnej informacji prawnej oraz edukacji prawnej społeczeństwa* (druk nr 3338), Warszawa, 25 maja 2015 r., Biuro Analiz Sejmowych Kancelaria Sejmu, http://orka.sejm.gov.pl/rexdomk7.nsf/Opdodr?OpenPage&nr=3338 (dostęp: 24 czerwca 2022 r.).

Wiaderek G. (ed.), *Poradnictwo prawne i obywatelskie – system, koszty, innowacje*, Warszawa 2014, https://www.academia.edu/8085878/Poradnictwo_prawne_i_obywatelskie_system_koszty_innowacje (access: 24.06.2022).

Wiaderek G., [in:] *System nieodpłatnego poradnictwa prawnego i obywatelskiego w Polsce. Propozycje rozwiązań modelowych i założeń polityki państwa*, Warszawa 2013, https://www.ekonomiaspoleczna.gov.pl/download/files/PPIO/System-nieodplatnego-ppio-w-polsce.pdf (access: 24.06.2022 r.).

Winczorek J., *Dostęp do poradnictwa. Stan obecny i możliwości zmiany*, [in:] *Poradnictwo prawne i obywatelskie – system, koszty, innowacje*, red. G. Wiaderek, Warszawa 2014.

Witkowska A., *Przegląd przepisów zawierających odniesienia dotyczące poradnictwa prawnego i obywatelskiego*, Warszawa 2012, source: http://www.inpris.pl/fileadmin/

user_upload/documents/pomoc_prawna/Przegl%C3%84%E2%80%A6d_przepis%C4%82%C5%82w_zawieraj%C3%84%E2%80%A6cych_odniesienia_dotycz%C3%84%E2%80%A6ce_pomocy_prawnej_i_obywatelskiej.pdf (access: 14.11.2020).

Other

Barendrecht M., *Rechtwijzer: Why Online Supported Dispute Resolution Is Hard to Implement*, Brottsoffrets rättigheter, źródło: https://www.nck.uu.se/kunskapsbanken/amnesguider/rattsvasendets-ansvar/brottsoffrets-rattigheter/ (access: 06.12.2022).

Bartnik A. S., Kowalska K. J., Krysztofowicz A., *Nieodpłatna pomoc prawna online w czasach epidemii*, LEX/el. 2020.

Fisher G., *Advice on Everything. A History of the Citizens Advice Service in Harrow, 1939–2009*, source: https://citizensadvice.citizensadvice.org.uk/harrow_cab_history.pdf (access: 24.11.2020).

Garlicki L., *Rola sędziego krajowego w procesie wykonywania orzeczeń Europejskiego Trybunału Praw Człowieka*, [in:] *IX Seminarium Warszawskie. Dysfunkcje polskiego prawa – jak poprawić system środków prawnych w Polsce?*, Warszawa 2016, source: https://www.gov.pl/web/dyplomacja/seminaria-warszawskie-publikacje (access: 21.12.2020).

Gierach E., *Kontrola jakości udzielanej nieodpłatnej pomocy prawnej* (text in the possession of the authors of the study).

International Legal Aid Group Conference, 14–16.06.2017.

General Comment No. 32: Article 14: Right to Equality before Courts and Tribunals and to Fair Trial, CCPR/C/GC/32

Informacja Najwyższej Izby Kontroli o wynikach kontroli. Funkcjonowanie systemu nieodpłatnej pomocy prawnej 2018, LOP 430.001.2018, Nr ew. 4/2018/P/17/090/LOP, dostęp: https://www.nik.gov.pl/plik/id,16874,vp,19432.pdf (dostęp: 6 grudnia 2021 r.).

Informacja o stanie przestrzegania wolności i praw człowieka i obywatela w 2017 r. oraz o działalności Rzecznika Praw Obywatelskich, p. 168, source: https://bip.brpo.gov.pl/pl/content/informacja-o-stanie-przestrzegania-wolnosci-i-praw-czlowieka-i-obywatela-w-2017-r-oraz-o (access: 22.12.2022).

Kieres L., *Sprawna administracja w orzecznictwie Trybunału Konstytucyjnego*, source: http://www.repozytorium.uni.wroc.pl/Content/79097/15_Kieres-L.pdf (access: 21.11.2020).

Ocena Ministra Sprawiedliwości z realizacji zadań z zakresu nieodpłatnej pomocy prawnej, nieodpłatnego poradnictwa obywatelskiego oraz edukacji prawnej za 2020 r.

Ocena Ministra Sprawiedliwości z realizacji zadań z zakresu nieodpłatnej pomocy prawnej, nieodpłatnego poradnictwa obywatelskiego oraz edukacji prawnej za 2021 rok.

Optional Protocol to the Convention on the Rights of the Child on the involvement of children in armed conflict, 25 May 2000 (Dz.U. z 2007 r. Nr 91, poz. 608) and Optional Protocol to the Convention on the Rights of the Child on the sale of children, child prostitution and child pornography, 25 May 2000 (Dz.U. z 2007 r. Nr 76, poz. 494).

Proposition 1981/82: 28, p. 12.

Regeringens proposition (Uzasadnienie do nowelizacji Instrumentu Rządzenia) 1996/97:9, p. 7.

Rządowy projekt ustawy o dostępie do nieodpłatnej pomocy prawnej przyznawanej przez państwo osobom fizycznym, Sejm V Kadencji, druk sejmowy nr 29, pp. 4–5. Source: http://orka.sejm.gov.pl/proc5.nsf/opisy/29.htm (access: 02.07.2022).

Stanowisko Prezydium Krajowej Rady Radców Prawnych z 9 października 2017 r. w sprawie przedstawionej przez Prezydenta RP nowelizacji ustawy z 5 sierpnia 2015 r. o nieodpłatnej pomocy prawnej i edukacji prawnej (druk sejmowy nr 1868), s. 4, source: https://orka.sejm.gov.pl/Druki8ka.nsf/0/4A58B025E60CA65DC12581B50033C036/%24File/1868-001.pdf (access: 22.12.2022).

Stanowisko Rzecznika Praw Obywatelskich zawarte w piśmie do Prezydenta RP w zakresie zakresu zmian w ustawie o nieodpłatnej pomocy prawnej: Pismo RPO IV.510.9.2014.AB, p. 3, source: https://bip.brpo.gov.pl/sites/default/files/Wyst%C4%85pienie%20do%20Prezydenta%20RP%20w%20sprawie%20nieodp%C5%82atnej%20pomocy%20prawnej.pdf (access: 22.12.2022 r.).

Tomuschat Ch, *International Covenant on Civil and Political Rights*, United Nations Audiovisual Library of International Law (access: https://legal.un.org/avl/pdf/ha/iccpr/iccpr_e.pdf, 18.07.2023)

Uchwała nr 79/2018 Prezydium Naczelnej Rady Adwokackiej z 19 czerwca 2018 r., p. 1; source http://www.adwokatura.pl/admin/wgrane_pliki/file-uchwala-nr-79-2018-23655.pdf (access: 28.06.2022).

Załącznik nr 3 Rekomendacje I Kongresu Praw Obywatelskich: Rekomendacja pt. „Pomoc w trudnych sytuacjach, w tym pomoc prawna" zamieszczona w informacji o stanie przestrzegania wolności i praw człowieka i obywatela w 2017 r. oraz o działalności Rzecznika Praw Obywatelskich.

Judgment of the Constitutional Court

Judgment of the Constitutional Court from 8 08 2016 r., K 37/13, OTK-A 2016, poz. 28.

Judgment of the Constitutional Court from 31 lipca 2015 r., K 41/12, OTK-A 2015, nr 7, poz. 102.

Judgment of the Constitutional Court from 29 08. 2006 r., SK 23/05, OTK-A 2006, nr 8, poz. 94.

Judgment of the Constitutional Court from 27.04.2005 r., P 1/05, OTK-A 2005, nr 4, poz. 42.

Judgment of the Constitutional Court from 11 05.2005 r., K 18/04, OTK-A 2005, nr 5, poz. 49.

Judgment of the Constitutional Court from 7 09. 2004 r., P 4/04, OTK-A 2004, nr 8, poz. 81.

Judgment of the Supreme Administrative Court

Judgment of the Supreme Administrative Court of April 27, 2021, II GSK 877/18, LEX No. 3184830.

Judgment of the Supreme Administrative Court of April 18, 2019, II FSK 1275/17, LEX No. 2694771.

Judgment of the Supreme Administrative Court of 15 czerwca 2018 r., I OSK 1187/18, LEX nr 2509132.

Judgment of the Supreme Administrative Court of 30.10.2002 r., II SA 1956/02, LEX nr 78062.

Judgment of the Supreme Administrative Court of 07.12.2010 r., II OSK 1774/10, CBOSA.

Others court rulings

Judgment of the ECHR *w sprawie Salduz przeciwko Turcji* z 27 listopada 2008 r. (skarga nr 36391/02).

Judgment of the WSA w Warsow from 26.04.2022 r., VII SA/Wa 2433/21, LEX nr 3407140.

Judgment of the WSA w Warsow from 27.05.2021 r., VII SA/Wa 593/21, LEX nr 3194742.

Judgment of the WSA w Warszawie z 04.05.2021 r., VII SA/Wa 2268/20, LEX nr 3265719.

Judgment of the WSA we Wrocław from 12.10.2017 r., IV SAB/Wr 115/17, LEX nr 2391598.

Judgment of the WSA we Wrocławiu z 25.05.2018 r., IV SAB/Wr 27/18, LEX nr 2510555.

Judgment of the WSA we Wrocławiu z 12.10.2017 r., IV SAB/Wr 115/17, LEX nr 2391598.

Judgment of the WSA w Poznaniu z 19 października 2017 r., II SAB/Po 47/16, LEX nr 2424828.

Order of the Supreme Court of January 14, 2021, II DK 15/21, LEX No. 3106152.

Ius, Lex et Res Publica

Studies in Law, Philosophy and Political Cultures

Edited by
Anna Jaron

Vol. 1 Anna Jaron: Socio-Economic Constitutional Rights in Democratisation Processes. An Account of the Constitutional Dialogue Theory. 2012.

Vol. 2 Stanisław Filipowicz: Democracy – The Power of Illusion. 2013.

Vol. 3 Teresa Dukiet-Nagórska (ed.): The Postulates of Restorative Justice and the Continental Model of Criminal Law. As Illustrated by Polish Criminal Law 2014.

Vol. 4 Agnieszka Kupzok: Enforcement of Patents on Geographically Divisible Inventions. An Inquiry into the Standard of Substantive Patent Law Infringement in Cross-Border Constellations. 2015.

Vol. 5 Alicja Jagielska-Burduk / Wojciech Szafrański: Legal Issues in Cultural Heritage Management. A Polish Perspective. 2016.

Vol. 6 Maciej Mataczyński (ed.): The Takeover of Public Companies as a Mode of Exercising EU Treaty Freedoms. 2017.

Vol. 7 Maciej Barczewski (ed.): Value of Information. Intellectual Property, Privacy and Big Data. 2018.

Vol. 8 Pawel Smoleń, Marcin Burzec: Introduction to Polish Tax Law. 2018.

Vol. 9 Łukasz Pohl, Konrad Burdziak: Judicial Interpretation of the 1997 Criminal Code Provisions on Self-Defence. 2019.

Vol. 10 Adam Szot: Judicial Review of Administrative Discretion. The Influence of Court Decisions on Administrative Actions. 2019.

Vol. 11 Michał Peno / Konrad Burdziak (eds.): The Concept of Modern Law. Polish and Central European Tradition. 2019.

Vol. 12 Leszek Leszczyński / Bartosz Liżewski / Adam Szot (eds.): Potential of Precedent in the Statutory Legal Order. 2019.

Vol. 13 Łukasz Bolesta: In Search of a Model for the Legal Protection of a Whistleblower in the Workplace in Poland. A legal and comparative study. 2020.

Vol. 14 Paweł Chmielnicki / Adam Sulikowski (eds.): New Perspectives on Legislation. A Comparative Approach. 2020.

Vol. 15 Marcin Burzec / Beata Kucia-Guściora / Paweł Smoleń: Agricultural Activity in Poland: A Fiscal and Legal Study. 2020.

Vol. 16 Magdalena Półtorak / Ilona Topa (eds.): Women, Children and (Other) Vulnerable Groups. Standards of Protection and Challenges for International Law. 2021.

Vol. 17 Josef Albert Fox: Die polnische Verfassung vom 3. Mai 1791. Hintergründe der Entstehung und der Außerkraftsetzung. Stellung Polens im Zeitalter der Aufklärung. 2021.

Vol. 18 Barbara Janusz-Pohl (ed.): Juvenile Justice Systems: Poland-Brazil-Portugal. 2021.

Vol. 19 Leszek Leszczyński: General Reference Clauses in the Judicial Process. Context of Legislative Intentions Interpretative Discretion. 2021.

Vol. 20 Francisco J. Campos Zamora: Das Problem der Begründung richterlicher Entscheidungen. Eine Analyse auf der Grundlage der Theorie der juristischen Argumentation. 2021.

Ius, Lex et Res Publica

Studies in Law, Philosophy and Political Cultures

Edited by

Barbara Janusz-Pohl and Anna Jaron

Vol. 21 Aneta Skorupa-Wulczyńska: Language Rights of the Citizen of the European Union. 2022.

Vol. 22 Mateusz Osiecki: International Legal Aspects of Aerial Terrorism. Methods of Law Enforcement in Avia-tion. 2022.

Vol. 23 Vladimír Sharp / Gabriela Blahoudková / Jakub Handrlica (eds.): Law, Pandemics and Ownership Restrictions. 2022.

Vol. 24 Piotr Kasprzyk / Anna Konert: Drones – Future of Aviation Law? Interference of Public Law in Private Law. 2023.

Vol. 25 Szymon Pawelec (ed.): Consensual Procedures in Criminal Law – Comparative Perspective. 2023.

Vol. 26 Dorota Pudzianowska: The Statelessness in Public Law. 2023.

Vol. 27 Bogusław Przywora / Aleksander Wróbel: Formalised Access to Pre-jurisdictional Free Legal Aid. Analysis based on Example of Ukraine, Poland, Great Britain and Sweden. 2023.

www.peterlang.com

www.ingramcontent.com/pod-product-compliance
Ingram Content Group UK Ltd.
Pitfield, Milton Keynes, MK11 3LW, UK
UKHW041827031026
15587UKWH00002B/611

9 783631 902585